Pilgrim's Digress

a journey around Britain and the soul

Don Egan

Copyright © Don Egan 2017

The right of Don Egan to be identified as author of this work has been asserted by him in accordance with the Copyright, Designs and Patents Act 1988.

ISBN-13: 978-1973703181
ISBN-10: 1973703181

For

Martin

Contents

1

Namasté

I could just tell you that I got in a car and went to some interesting places, and met some interesting people. But that wouldn't be the true story of this journey.

I did get in the car and drive more than 2,700 miles, and that is what this book is about. But I never planned to do that until some stuff happened.

Think about it. I drove from my house... to... my house... by the longest and most inconvenient route.

Who does that? And why?

It began through a conversation with my friend.

'It's all about the journey, Don. It's never really about the destination – always the journey,' said Martin.

He'd said that many times before but I was slow to accept his wisdom. I was usually glad to get the journey over with and reach my destination. But I think he was on to something. He usually was.

Martin was my closest man-friend. How do you measure that? I don't really know, but he was the one I could be myself with. There was no hidden agenda or competition. We were not going to stab each other in the back or betray each other. We had both shared our darkest moments and looked out for each other.

It was a strange but beautiful friendship – Martin was a complete extrovert, always ready to encounter new situations with little or no preparation. I, on the other hand, am far closer to the introvert end of the scale, always wanting to think and plan every move carefully. Yet, somehow, because of our differences, we had a remarkable synergy and sparked off each other in a very creative way. Many of the books I've written began life as a conversation with Martin. Added to this mix was the fact we were both slightly mad. I still am.

On this particular day, we were walking along the clifftop at Flamborough Head, in Yorkshire. I'd been sharing another idea for a book with Martin. I was thinking of travelling to different parts of Britain and spending a little time with people of different outlooks on life and different kinds of spiritual journey.

I find the story of people's journey in life fascinating – the things that inspire and direct us in ways that form us into better people who then, in turn, make the world a better place.

Martin and I chatted about various other things as we walked, although you could never have a real 'walk' with Martin – it was always what I think bird-watchers call a 'stop-start'. A 'stop-start' is a walk that has frequent stops to look through binoculars, for wildlife. Martin was not only a birdwatcher; he was a proper ornithologist who was at the top of his game. 'Twitchers' from all over the world would have paid good money to be in my place on the cliffs at Flamborough Head that day. His blog, Birding Frontiers, was getting millions of hits from around the globe. However, our walk was for friendship not birdwatching, at least for me. Martin was always looking for birds – that was a given. But he could do that on autopilot and still have a conversation about other things as he did it.

He also talked about his cancer and how it was now terminal. He never wanted to talk about it too much but loved to talk about other things. But now it wasn't so much about if he would die prematurely, but more about how long he had left to live.

Never before have I encountered another human squeezing every last drop of fun and goodness and learning out of life, as I did during those days with Martin.

'I'm looking for the 'gold' in every day,' he said, as each new day was seen as a very precious gift.

As we got back to his house, and I was preparing to leave for the five-hour journey back to Suffolk, he caught my arm.

'You've got to do it!' he said. 'That book idea. Driving around the country and meeting people – you must do it, Don.'

That was the last time Martin walked with me. The cancer spread and soon he lost the ability to walk. The next time we went anywhere near the cliffs at Flamborough, I pushed Martin in a wheelchair. It was so not him! He was 'Mr Outdoors', 'Mr Active'. Yet he continued with the stop-start, binoculars in hand, and still spotting various birds as they arrived in the UK from some far flung land.

And, not long after the wheelchair walk, Martin became pretty much confined to bed. My visits were then to his bedside.

Sadly, Martin passed away in January 2016, a few days after his 52nd birthday.

I had the honour of speaking at Martin's funeral. I was a broken wreck inside. His loss was obviously devastating for his family. For me, it felt like having my right arm amputated. Martin was the one who had kept me sane over recent years. Now he was gone.

I am very familiar with grief and loss. They've been a bit of a theme in my life. My Mum suddenly died when she was in her mid-fifties. Our son was born with a major heart defect a few months later. Then my Dad suddenly died in his mid-fifties too. A while later, our son died shortly before his third birthday. I've lost other close friends over the years. Every loss took its toll. But losing Martin hit me very hard. Maybe it stirred up all the old grief and loss.

Eventually, with the help of friends and family, and a wonderful counsellor, I came through the season of grief to a more stable place.

As I reflected about the way we grieve when we lose close friends and family, I wondered what it is that hits us so hard. For me it seems to be that it's only through relationships with others that we truly discover ourselves. If we are, in fact, created in the image of God, I don't think we'll find God by looking in the mirror and admiring ourselves. I think we find God in each other.

Obviously, I don't want to make out that Martin was some sort of deity – it's not that at all. But I saw in him, as I do in others, some aspects of God's nature. There were moments when he was as mad as a box of frogs. But there were also moments of tremendous grace, humility, and love. It's in those moments that we can catch a glimpse of something of the divine in each other.

I think Hindus have understood something that most of us miss here. Their simple but profound greeting – Namasté – sums up what I mean.

Namasté is usually spoken with a slight bow and hands pressed together, palms touching and fingers pointing upwards, thumbs close to the chest. This gesture is called Añjali Mudrā or Pranamasana. In Hinduism it means 'I bow to the divine in you'. The greeting may also be spoken without the gesture, or the gesture performed wordlessly, carrying the same meaning.

The idea is quite foreign to our Western culture, although I think James Cameron illustrated it well in his blockbuster movie, *Avatar*. The phrase, *'I see you,'* in that film was in a similar vein.

I also think Jesus taught his followers the same thing.

'I have said you are gods'.
Jesus of Nazareth

I think there maybe something of the divine spark in every human soul, if we will just take the time to be quiet and observe.

Above all, I guess it was this light, this life, this 'gold', that I saw in the life of my friend that I was grieving for. It was so painful to lose him.

Life continued to bring the usual mix of joys and further sorrows during the time of mourning, but everything was stitched with the colour of loss.

The idea of the book and the journey that we'd talked about got lost and forgotten in all of that.

One thing I have worked out over the years is that, if an idea is 'true' – by which I mean that it's not so much your idea of what to do with your life, as life's idea of what it will do with you – then it will come back again. Deep calls to deep, and God, or the Universe, or whatever, draws you onward on your own journey.

2

The small voice

Part of my creativity in life has involved listening to a small voice inside me. Not that I hear voices, you understand, but I sometimes feel a 'pull' in a certain direction.

Imagine a blind man flying a kite. How will he know that the kite is still flying? Perhaps his friends tell him. But what happens when he is flying his kite alone, enjoying a rare moment of solitude? How will he know if the kite is still flying at those times?

'I can feel the pull on the string,' he explains.

That is how I hear this small voice that has led me through life thus far – I feel the pull.

Sometimes I don't feel anything and then I know 'the kite' is on the ground. Nothing is flying.

A couple of years back I began to feel this pull – to hear this small quiet voice gently drawing me. It was hard to make out what I was being pulled towards but ideas began to form in my mind – a journey, a wander. Meeting people and chatting about life and spirituality seemed to be part of it, but also solitude and reflection too. The journey would be geographical but also an inner journey.

The idea was put on the backburner for a couple of years owing to several very difficult situations in our family and among our friends, not least after Martin, my closest friend, died. In fact, for all intents and purposes it was completely forgotten.

However, towards the end of 2016 I felt the pull again – the small quiet voice was speaking about it. I thought perhaps I would make a start and go on several short journeys throughout 2017.

Then, as usually happens when I give attention to the small voice, the idea began to develop.

'Couldn't you do it all in one journey?' asked my counsellor. She has a wonderful way of asking significant questions. She had helped me through the minefield of bereavement after Martin passed away, and I'd shared the possibility of doing something with the idea.

She was just asking but it was a great question. I'd not even considered such a possibility. I thought about that question for a week and began to think that not only could it be done in one journey, but that it may be far better if it was.

Then another question began creeping into my thoughts – what destinations or locations would this journey involve?

As I thought about that question I felt the 'pull' to visit certain locations around the country. Some had a spiritual meaning, and some a sort of sentimental significance. As I thought about these places, I realised there were other places in Britain, that I had not yet visited, that could be of interest on this journey.

And so I began to pencil in a route of geographical locations I wanted to visit. These were so widespread that I hit on the idea of a journey from my home in Suffolk, down to Land's End, then journeying around the country, up to John O'Groats on the North coast of Scotland and eventually meandering back South East to Suffolk.

Some locations were chosen simply for their photogenic qualities. Others were chosen for being somehow spiritually or historically significant.

As I began to share a little of this mad idea, conversations threw up significance and meaning to some of the places I was already planning to visit. Again the 'pull' or the small voice seemed to be drawing me on a certain journey.

The idea now seemed a sort of madness but I have benefited greatly from being a bit mad over the years. It makes life interesting.

'If we don't go mad once in a while, there's no hope.'
Rachel Joyce - *The Unlikely Pilgrimage of Harold Fry*

Eventually I had to start thinking about the very practical nature of this journey – times, dates, route and accommodation along the way, not to mention the cost.

'But what are you doing? What is the purpose?' – these questions came from others but also inside my own head.

In many ways it makes no sense whatsoever to travel the longest route, without crossing the sea, from your own home and back to your own home. It's an unnecessary journey. Why not just stay at home and save yourself a lot of money and inconvenience?

Good question. And yet, I feel the 'pull'. The small voice draws me to the journey.

Spiritually and emotionally, it became a very necessary journey.

It is often through unexpected journeys, or detours, that we find out new things about ourselves. I was not setting out to 'find myself', nor was I trying to draw close to God. I think I found myself a while ago. And I generally feel close to God, though not always that he is close to me. He's a bit like that, I think.

Even so, on a journey, we discover new things, often about ourselves, and we're the better for it, however tortured the journey may be.

So, I decided that, sometime in the first half of 2017, I would get in the car and drive and stop and walk and take photos and think and walk and drive some more. At some stage I'll arrive back home. But, by then, I expect home and I will have changed.

3

Just do it

'It's a dangerous business, Frodo, going out your door.
You step onto the road, and if you don't keep your feet,
there's no knowing where you might be swept off to.'
J.R.R. Tolkien, *The Lord of the Rings*

Day 1 – Monday
Stowmarket – Reading – Exeter

I'd been preparing for this trip for weeks. I'd done my usual thing of trying to think of all eventualities – I'd organised clothes and camping equipment, bought gadgets and storage boxes, timed routes to all the places I planned to visit, and even made a sleeping platform to fit in the back of the car (hotels would be too expensive, but I hate sleeping under canvas).

I reckoned the trip would take about three weeks, but I wanted it to be a little open ended to allow the journey to take a slightly different direction if it needed to.

Despite all the preparations, I still went into 'headless chicken mode' on departure day, throwing last minute things into the back of the car and nearly forgetting to get fuel.

That done, I was just about to set off when I realised I hadn't contacted a campsite down in Devon, where I would be sleeping that night. I looked up a couple on my phone and gave one of them a call.

'We're not doing tents this week because the field is too wet. But we're open for caravans,' the lady said.

'I'll be sleeping in my car, if that's OK,' I replied.

'Oh. Yes. I suppose that'll be alright then. Just come up to the house when you arrive. I'll be here.'

It was that simple.

I had several moments of panic during this setting off process, where I almost threw in the towel and abandoned the trip, as it seemed completely mad and unnecessary. But I know that a journey of a thousand miles begins with the first step, as they say. Or, in my case, a journey of 2,700 miles begins with starting the car and driving out of a Tesco car park.

oOo

I'm not sure which journey disturbed me the most – the geographical one, with the idea of sleeping in the car, or the inner journey and how I would feel throughout this mad endeavour.

As I hesitated between abandoning the whole trip and just getting on with it, a familiar slogan came to mind.

Just do it.

You've probably read or heard that phrase many times. It's the slogan of the shoe company, Nike - a slogan that helped them to become a global brand. The slogan was first floated in 1988 at a meeting about marketing their products.

Just do it.

How many people have launched into a potentially frightening task by repeating the Nike slogan?

I have used it in my own head in many difficult situations.

Think of all the marathon runners, about to attempt what seems impossible, who, just before the starting line, whisper to themselves, 'Just do it!' If you're wearing Nike trainers to run your marathon, how could you not think that before you start off?

What I didn't know at the time was that the slogan is credited to a convicted murderer.

Gary Gilmore was the first person in the United States to be executed after the reinstatement of the death penalty in 1976. He had brutally murdered two people even though they had complied with his commands.

He was executed by a firing squad on 17 January 1977. When asked for any last words, Gilmore simply replied, 'Let's do it.'

The advertising agency guy adjusted Gilmore's words to 'Just do it,' and the rest, as they say, is history.

Now here I was, about to launch myself into the unknown.

Yes.

Come on Egan!

Just do it!

I started the engine and, though I felt unprepared, I decided to just do it.

oOo

I'd arranged a rendezvous with my old friend Catharine in Reading that first day, then onwards to meet my brother in Exeter. At first, the trip seemed very familiar. From Suffolk, so many of my journeys involve the A14 to A11 to M11 to M25.

I've done more airport runs, along this route, to Heathrow than I care to remember. The further journey down to Exeter to see my little brother, Simon, is not unfamiliar either.

I'd thought of 'popping in' to see Catharine in Reading on several trips but, on a specific trip to somewhere, we often can't spare the time.

However, despite my aversion to improvisation when travelling, this trip lends itself to detours. Although meeting someone at Reading Services is not a detour at all. It was very much on the way.

I've known Catharine since she was a young child, becoming friends with her parents when I was eighteen years old.

It occurred to me that I hadn't thought through the meeting-up-with-people thing. Should I have an agenda or a set of questions? Or should I just meet people and see what happens? I think the friendships I like most are those with people who don't turn up to coffee with a planned agenda. I much prefer just meeting, chatting, and seeing what transpires.

As I approached Reading Services, I found myself

dropping into the middle of a long military convoy of about eight or nine very large vehicles. It turned out they were coming off at Reading Services too. My little 4x4 was dwarfed by the huge dark green convoy. I managed to peel off and find the car park.

Catharine was sitting at a table near the entrance, and soon we were reminiscing about old times, particularly when she had joined one of our teams going out to Africa, visiting Uganda and Rwanda. She was preparing to be ordained in the Church of England at the time, but took a couple of weeks out of her schedule to join us on the life-changing trip. She's now been ordained for many years.

Inevitably, she asked me what my trip was about. I explained some of the things that had led me to embark on this journey, but also admitted I was still unsure about what I was doing.

I guess it was a bit like her coming with me on a journey into the unknown when she came to Africa. I was very used to taking people out to Africa for their first encounter with the continent. I was always able to guide or reassure people as they went through the inevitable culture shock.

But now I was on a journey into the unknown – not into the wilds of Africa, but in my own country. I had no real guide except the 'inner voice' or listening to my heart.

It was great to catch up with Catharine after such a long time and also to have this first meet-up of the trip.

Soon it was time to get back on the road to reach Exeter and my younger brother. We said goodbye and took a 'selfie' for the blog I was writing about my daily encounters. Catharine wished me well as I travelled.

I set the satnav for Exmouth, the place where I would camp on the first night. I thought I'd go and check-in there first, and then go into Exeter to meet my brother Simon.

As I drove, I thought about the spiritual event of 'going out into the wilderness.' This event is evident in many stories throughout history. Buddha left his palace. Mohammed meditated in remote caves. Jesus went out into the wilderness and faced the temptation of the Devil.

But this journey also shows up in the lives of lesser mortals. St Anthony went out into the desert to be alone for fourteen years. He later became the father of modern monasticism. St Cuthbert lived for many years as a hermit on Holy Island.

At certain times in their life, some men and women go off on a journey into the 'wilderness'. Of course, the 'wilderness' is not always a desert place but may just be a place that is far removed from their usual day-to-day life.

It's interesting that in the stories of historical figures, and those of ordinary men and women, it is often out in their 'desert place' that they find a new clarity about the direction their life should go. Others speak of hearing the 'voice of God' in those moments. Somehow, when we silence the noisy voices of our everyday life, we may hear the gentle voice of God.

The idea of pilgrimage, to a spiritually significant place, or going on a spiritual journey, carries the same idea. The word 'pilgrimage' literally means 'through the fields'. The pilgrim's journey normally involves walking to a special place of significance. I was doing it differently – by driving in my car and visiting many places and people. But it was nevertheless a sort of pilgrimage, or going out into the 'desert'.

oOo

A couple of hours later, I passed by Exeter and was guided onto the road to Exmouth. I found the campsite and went up to the house as instructed. A man answered the door.

'Are you the guy that's sleeping in his car?' he asked.

'Yes that's me.'

'My wife's just popped out but she left this note – "Man sleeping in his car. Tell him to park in plot 1",' he said. 'She'll come and find you tonight or tomorrow.'

Unfortunately, when I got to the camping area, someone was parked on plot 1. I saw a couple of people doing some work on the grounds, and I asked if they knew whose car it was.

'Oh that's Dave's car. We'll get him to move it.'

Well, I didn't have time to wait for Dave as I needed to get into Exeter and find Simon. Hopefully Dave would have moved it when I got back.

It was great to be meeting my brother, Simon, on the first day of my trip. Some years ago, Simon walked The Way of St James, also known as The Camino de Santiago – or just The Camino, for short. The Camino is not short though. It's a 500-mile route across Spain, and Simon walked every one of those miles. It was a life-changing experience for him.

Today, Simon lives in St Sidwell's Church in Exeter. I think there is a little chapel still there, but now the building has a community centre on the ground floor, and flats on the first floor.

St Sidwell, or Sidwella as she was known, was a young devout woman who lived during the Roman occupation. Her wicked stepmother arranged for her head to be chopped off with a worker's scythe, while Sidwella was praying in a cornfield. At the spot where Sidwella's head came to rest, a spring of water rose up, which was found to have healing properties. So the place became a place of pilgrimage and healing.

I found Simon, and we walked into town. We went by Exeter Cathedral and had a look at the ancient hotel, opposite the Cathedral, that had recently burnt down. On the way to find somewhere to eat, we passed several rough sleepers who were sheltering in shop doorways or little alleyways in the city – a growing number of the poor and vulnerable slipping through the welfare net.

Simon and I ordered a meal and chatted. It's always good to see Simon. He, too, was curious as to what I was doing but, as a fellow 'explorer', was not surprised by my trip. I told him some of the events that had led up to this mad journey. We talked about all sorts of stuff and then it was time for me to head back to the campsite to set up the 'car-camper'. We walked back to Simon's place and then I drove back to the campsite at Exmouth.

oOo

Thankfully 'Dave' had moved his car so I parked in Plot 1 as requested. I'd had this romantic idea of getting the folding chair out of the car, having a glass of wine, and watching the sunset. But the day was overcast. It had started to rain and it was already going dark. The temperature had dropped too.

There were half a dozen caravans on site but most seemed unoccupied, and the ones that were occupied had the curtains drawn and lights on.

I opened the car door and looked at the 'bed' and the boxes of clothes and equipment that pretty much filled up the car.

How the heck was I even going to fit in here? Why had I not done a trial run before the trip to iron out problems?

I must have stood staring into the car for about two minutes just amazed by my own stupidity. What had I been thinking? There was no way I could even get into the car to reach the 'bed' with all the storage boxes I had. My heart sank.

Very soon the declining temperature and increasing rain urged me to sort out the situation.

Right. What's the best I can do tonight?

I found a torch and switched it on. I started opening the plastic storage boxes to find night stuff to sleep in. Let's find my Kindle – I'll do some bedtime reading, I thought.

In the end, I sorted out the absolute minimum.

I went off to the toilet block on the campsite armed with my toothbrush and toothpaste.

On my return, I stacked as many of the storage boxes as I could onto the front seats, which created a little bit of space. (People have asked why I didn't just get in the car through the tailgate. You had to be there. It's a 4x4 and quite high off the ground. And then the bed-platform makes it even more impractical).

I set up my camping lamp in the car and climbed in through the rear passenger door.

I was now squashed almost into a fetal position and could barely turn round. Maybe I should have got changed in the toilet block.

Imitating Harry Houdini as I tried to get changed, I got really angry with myself. What a really stupid idea this was! Sleeping in the car! You silly, stupid man! You're nearly 60 years old and you have evidently failed to grow up!

Then I started laughing. For a moment a saw the unfolding scene as a spectator would. Yes. It was a really silly idea but it was quite funny too.

A few minutes later, I'd got changed for bed without pulling a muscle or breaking a window. I'd blacked out the rear windows with custom made panels covered with off cuts from a black sheet. I draped the remainder of the black sheet over the two front-seat headrests for a little privacy.

As I tried to get to sleep, I thought about the day. I thought about the rough-sleepers in Exeter that Simon and I had passed tonight. I may have been struggling with sleeping in my adapted car, but I was dry, sheltered, and warm. At any time, I could opt-out of my self-imposed situation. The homeless cannot do that. They were stuck there, sleeping in cold doorways trying to protect their bedding from rain, possibly fearful of attack or abuse from late-night drunks.

I was also aware that it was the beginning of Lent – a time when people of faith deny themselves some personal comfort. I used to fast in Lent, on Wednesdays and Fridays – no food until 9pm - back in the early 1980s. I hadn't done any self-denial stuff since then. Maybe this simple night of sleeping in the car, with few comforts, would be good for the soul. Or maybe I'd just have a terrible night's sleep and regret the whole thing.

New spiritual seasons, or chapters, tend to begin with some sort of awakening. Our heart seems drawn to some new experience. The old ways and rituals lose their meaning and the soul becomes hungry for some new, or deeper, encounter.

Those around us may misunderstand what we are doing. They may think we have lost our faith or given up. As we ourselves are uncertain exactly where it is that we are going, it is impossible to explain without sounding extremely vague. Much like the metamorphosis of a caterpillar becoming a butterfly, so the soul seems to die and become lifeless for a season. But it does not die. It stills itself as it lets go of the past. Inside the chrysalis it gathers itself and prepares to adapt to completely new ways of seeing the world.

The awakening actually begins with what looks like sleeping or death. The letting go of the old ways looks like a lying down to retire or rest. But strangely, it is the first stage in a new season.

4

Listening

"Inner guidance is heard like soft music in the night
by those who have learned to listen."
Vernon Howard

Day 2 – Tuesday
Exeter – Penzance – Lands End – Liskeard

Before I set off on this journey, my youngest daughter
lent me a book – *The Alchemist* by Paul Coelho. The
book tells the story of a young shepherd boy who learns
to listen. He listens to his sheep – not their bleating,
but their 'life-force' as it were. He then leaves his
sheep, and goes on a quest to a faraway land. There he
learns that he must also listen to the wind, the camels,
and even the desert, in order to be safely guided to his
treasure.

This idea of listening to nature, and to the Earth, has
been lost in our modern culture. It may still be found
in ancient cultures in the Middle East, among Native
Americans, and in parts of Africa.

For most of us in the West, we are so constantly bombarded by the voices of advertising, social media, radio, and TV, that we never hear the gentle voice of nature, the Universe, or the still small voice of God – call it what you will.

Jesus, the carpenter from Nazareth, spoke about it too.

'The wind blows wherever it pleases. You hear its sound, but you cannot tell where it comes from or where it is going. So it is with everyone born of the Spirit.'

Today will be a day of listening, then.

I reached out and managed to open the car door. Then I rolled over and sort of somersaulted or, more accurately, fell out of the car into the crisp morning air. Thankfully there were no witnesses to this spectacle.

I opened the tailgate and pulled out my homemade 'table'. One end sat on the back of the car, the other on a foldout leg that stood on the ground. I pulled out the camping stove and water container and got the kettle going. Then I found some cereal and a pint of milk and had that. Soon the kettle boiled and I made a coffee. It was definitely a cold start to the day so I found my hat and pulled it on.

A lone camper emerged from one of the caravans and walked up to the toilet block. On his way back he stopped and said hello. He commented on my car-camper set up and I explained about my end-to-end journey. I was still feeling anxious about this trip but he just smiled.

'I did that sleeping in the car when I was younger,' he said. 'But I've got the caravan now.'

He told me he'd taken three weeks just to tour Scotland, but I was planning to my whole trip around Britain in under three weeks.

'I love it,' he said. 'I loved it so much I never went home. I rented my house out and I live in the caravan now. I've even met a young lady.'

I couldn't imagine permanently giving up my home and living in a caravan, but there was something about this stranger. He was making me feel more peaceful about my journey and the idea of just letting things unfold.

Eventually, he realised he was running late for meeting someone, and went off.

I stood finishing my coffee and looking across the field at the early morning mist. Interesting how chatting to a stranger had brought me peace about my journey. Also that he had car-camped when he was younger and had now found such peace with life on the road, it had become his preferred way of living.

If I was going to try 'listening to the spirit' or listening to my heart, I'd say my conversation with the stranger that morning was almost like a messenger had been sent to reassure me I was on the right track.

I washed up and got changed for the day ahead, and then moved all the boxes from the front seats into the back of the car.

I'd thought I'd go back into Exeter and have a coffee with Simon but time had slipped by. I looked at the planned route. I was aiming to meet my cousin's daughter Sam for lunch in Penzance, then heading to Land's End hoping to end up at Lizard Point for the night.

I decided to head straight for Land's End, to tick that off, and then back to Penzance to meet Sam.

I sent Simon a text to say I was pressing on with the journey.

I packed everything up and set the satnav for Land's End. Unfortunately there was a massive hold up with almost an hour delay as two really huge oversized loads had to come through roadworks I was queuing to get through, in the opposite direction. I realised I didn't have time to reach Land's End and get back to Penzance in time to meet Sam. Once the roadblock was passed I headed straight for Penzance. Sam messaged me the address of a nice cafe in a park and soon I'd found it, but parking was difficult. I drove a bit further to the seafront and found a car park there.

I was very aware I had an expensive laptop and expensive camera and other equipment in the car but I didn't want to keep carrying all that stuff with me every time I left the car. As I said, the back windows and the rear window were blacked out so you couldn't see all the stuff in the back of the car. I decided to risk it and leave it there.

I walked back up to the park and found the cafe. Moments later, Sam arrived – a friendly face. We ordered a couple of BLTs and some coffee.

Sam is an accomplished singer, musician and performer, as well as a mum to her two boys, and all round good person.

She asked about the journey and I realised I may probably have this conversation with most people I met. But, however much I tried to explain it, I was never really sure myself what I was doing.

I told Sam that I had discovered that a couple of places I was visiting on this journey were places where the ashes of significant friends had been scattered.

'I'll go and say goodbye to them,' I said.

Sam smiled.

'You could. Or you could go and say hello,' she said.

I really liked that idea.

If this is a day of listening, then that was a message right there.

Yes. Why not go and say 'Hello' instead of 'Goodbye'?

Soon it was time to get back on the road. I said goodbye to Sam, and walked back down to the seafront.

It was windy but the sun had come out a bit, so I thought I'd get the big camera out of the car, and take some photos of the coastline. I couldn't remember which box I'd put the camera in but after shuffling a few boxes around I found it. It started to rain a bit, as the wind picked up, so I found my waterproof coat and put that on.

I walked to the edge of the seafront and took a few photos. I walked further down the promenade and took a few more pictures.

The rain got heavier so I headed back to the car. When I got back to the car park I was shocked to see I'd left the car door wide open. All my stuff was on show to any passer-by – my laptop, iPad etc. What an idiot! I really must pay attention to what I'm doing. Thankfully nothing had been taken.

I got in the car and set off towards Land's End.

oOo

The only real reason I was even going to Land's End was that when I planned out the people and places I wanted to go and see, they were so spread out that I thought I'd make it a LE-JOG trip – Land's End to John O'Groats. It's highly unlikely I'll ever walk or cycle it, as most 'end-to-enders' do, but I could drive it.

I'd read that Land's End was highly commercialised and it was £5 just to park the car. I didn't want any of that – I just wanted to see Land's End. I pressed on with low expectations.

As I approached Land's End, I came to the 'First and Last Inn' and stopped to take a few photos. It was 'out of season' and there weren't many people about.

I drove on to Land's End and paid £3 to park. The landscape is pretty much ruined by the 'Land's End Experience', which I had absolutely no interest in. I was hoping to get a selfie at the famous Land's End sign, but even this has been chained off and there's a £9.99 charge to have your photo taken there.

The wind was blowing a gale as I walked down to the First and Last House in England. Here there were a few more tourists braving the elements. An American guy was loudly reading every sign to his family – I assumed all his family were illiterate, for some reason, and couldn't read the signs themselves.

A young Japanese couple were laughing and taking photos every five yards.

The rain started up again and I didn't want to get any wetter. I headed back up the hill to the car park. By the time I reached the car it was pouring down and I got soaked.

Inside the car I had a look at the rest of the route I'd planned for the day.

Hmmm. I had planned to go to Prussia Cove, just beyond Marazion, to get an atmospheric photo of St Michael's Mount. But by the time I got to Marazion, the weather was so bad you could hardly see St Michael's Mount from there. It would be invisible from Prussia Cove.

I pulled into a car park and squinted to see the Mount through the rain. I had fond memories of summertime trips here and walking across to the Mount, which is only possible at low tide. The photography part of the trip was going down the pan rapidly.

Then I thought about camping in this howling gale. Lizard Point is the most Southern point of Britain, so it would be even wetter and windier than here.

Listen... to your heart... the wind... God... I thought.

After a few minutes of 'listening', I decided to cut out part of the route and head inland, towards Brentnor Church. I wasn't due to reach there for a couple of days but maybe the weather was dryer and calmer further inland. And maybe the wind or the universe was redirecting me for some reason.

I read that Brentnor Church sits at the top of a cliff in stunning scenery. An internet search brought up amazing photos of the place. Legend has it that the people of Brentnor built their church but, in the night, the devil moved it up to the top of the cliff because he didn't want people to go.

The route involved a lot of small lanes and village roads, where the speed limit kept reducing to 30mph.

Time was getting on and I realised I wouldn't make it to Brentnor before dark. I started looking for campsites. This is when I found out that most campsites don't open until Easter – a slight flaw in my plan to car-camp!

I pulled over in a village to search for a B&B on my phone. Unfortunately, my phone had 'No Service'. No problem, I thought. I have prepared for this eventuality by installing Wi-Fi in my car. I switched on the car Wi-Fi... 'No Service'.

What now?

The rain was getting heavier and it was now starting to go dark. Then I remembered that my satnav has an accommodation section. I looked it up.

There was a Premier Inn in Liskeard about half an hour away. Unfortunately, this is the worst possible way to book a room with them. It was more than £80 for the room only, and extra if I wanted breakfast. By now I was so tired and worn out, I paid up. I had run out of options and I guess that's what they rely on.

oOo

I changed into some fresh clothes, and wrote up the blog post for the day. Then I went down to the restaurant to get some food. I ordered a nice gammon with egg and chips and a pint of something cold. And then it began.

There were a couple of guys on the table behind me and one of them was a loud-talker. You know, the sort of person you can hear from the other end of a crowded pub. His friend may have spoken once or twice, but all I could hear was the loud-talker with a hint of an American accent.

The American guy began every statement with the phrase, 'But the reality is...'

Then he changed it to 'See, here's the thing...' for the next five minutes.

Next, it was, 'That's what I'm saying.'

We came full circle back to 'But the reality is...'

But the reality is, he talks too loud. And here's the thing – I don't think his friend was interested in what he was selling. That's what I'm saying.

I tried to filter out the annoying loud-talker as I enjoyed my meal. But the reality is, that was hard to do. That's what I'm saying.

I finished my meal and sat back to finish my drink. Now he was so loud I could actually hear every word over the chatter of the crowded restaurant. I realised he was trying to browbeat his friend into accepting his version of Christianity. And what a very narrow, judge-mental and dogmatic version it was. He was not only not taking 'No' for an answer, he really wasn't listening to anything his friend was saying by way of objection, or to his questions.

I was quickly feeling on the side of his friend. What an idiot! So he wants his friend to 'find Jesus'. What is Jesus famous for? Maybe showing immense grace and love to the least, the last, and the lost. Jesus listened to the poor and blessed them. But this guy displayed no signs of the grace and love he was allegedly trying to promote. Quite the opposite. I, and I think everyone else sitting nearby, was getting really irritated by him. If anyone was showing grace and gentleness, it was his friend, who miraculously had resisted punching him in the mouth.

See here's the thing, the reality is, I went to bed early because I couldn't stand listening anymore.

That's what I'm saying.

Silence.

Listening.

It's quite important.

Solitude brings perspective.

There is a purpose to this trip.

oOo

Most of us are searching for a creed to believe, a song to sing, a flag to follow. For a season, we may find our tribe. We feel we belong with this community. We embrace their stories and their narratives.

But when the day comes when the creed seems hollow, the song sounds out of tune, and the flag seems threadbare, we are possibly being drawn towards a different tribe. And if it is God who calls us, we should follow. The way forward is not straight or easy though. We may try to hold on to what we know – those things that have worked well for us in the past. Even though they now seem hollow and don't really work, they are at least familiar.

But if we are ever to take hold of the new thing, whatever it may be, we have to let go of the old. Until we let go of the old thing, we can never embrace the new thing.

The new thing though, may be shrouded in mist – it's as yet unknown, and therefore requires faith to take hold of it.

Letting go of the familiar things can be frightening before we see what the future holds. But we have to pass through the darkness of metamorphosis.

'I tell you the truth, unless a grain of wheat falls to the ground and dies, it remains only a single seed. But if it dies, it produces many seeds.'

Jesus of Nazareth

Be careful who you listen to because they'll always be a donkey telling a racehorse how to run faster.

5

Hide and seek

'Goin' up to the spirit in the sky
That's where I'm gonna go when I die
When I die and they lay me to rest
Gonna go to the place that's the best.'
Norman Greenbaum - *Spirit In The Sky*

Day 3 – Wednesday
Liskeard – Brentnor – Stonehenge – Glastonbury

During breakfast at the hotel, I got a reply from my friend Diana, who I was hoping to meet in Glastonbury. I'd messaged and told her I'd be passing through a day earlier but she had a busy program and couldn't change the day. No problem. I'll just change the route a bit.

I could head over to Brentnor Church, and then over to Stonehenge, where I was originally going after meeting Diana. But I could do Stonehenge today and then come back on myself a bit.

Having realised that very few campsites were going to be open until Easter, I looked online for a B&B at Glastonbury for this evening. I booked into one and then packed up, and checked out.

The roads were cloaked in fine drizzle and the early morning fog had not cleared. On the way to find Brentnor Church, the fog got thicker until visibility was down to only a few yards.

The satnav got me to Brentnor Church car park. The church location should have been pretty obvious, as the church sits right on top of a cliff and can be seen for miles around. However, the thick fog hid it from sight. To be honest, I could barely see the other side of the small car park. I wandered around a bit in the rain but couldn't see a signpost for the footpath up to the church. On a clear day, there was probably no need for a signpost. But this was not a clear day.

I tried to use Google Maps on my phone so I could find the way up, but the location is remote and both my phone and the car Wi-Fi were 'No Service'.

Wandering around was just getting me wetter and wetter. Bearing in mind that I had only come here to take a stunning landscape photo, the odds were all against it. Even if I found the way up, there would be no chance of the photo unless I wanted a photo of fog.

I got back in the car and thought again. I looked at my overall plan for the trip. I thought it was probably best to head up to Stonehenge as time was passing, and I had to reach Glastonbury by this evening.

I set off through various degrees of fog and rain and eventually found Stonehenge. I had seen it from a distance a few times when driving down to Cornwall but I'd never actually visited before.

On my arrival at the car park, I was a bit shocked to read that it was £16.50 for adult admission. I was very pleased when I found that National Trust members get in for free. Glad I bought my membership card with me.

I arrived about the same time as two coaches – one was full of French teenagers and the other one full of Japanese tourists. I was an ethnic minority.

I caught the shuttle bus up to the stones and had a wander round. I hadn't realised it was surrounded by ancient burial mounds. It seemed it was important to these ancient people to be buried within sight of this place. Was it an ancient place of worship? Or was it an elaborate clock, marking the summer solstice? A week earlier it had taken me nearly an hour to change the clock on our oven, when the clocks went forward for British Summertime. How the heck you put Stonehenge an hour forward I've no idea.

It's an interesting place. I kept coming back to thinking about the burial mounds. It's fascinating what humans do with their dead. And, often, what we believe dictates what we do with the remains of the departed.

Early beliefs were that when someone dies they are buried and descend into the shadowy place of the dead, which was believed to be under the ground. Therefore burying them makes sense.

In the Old Testament of the Bible, this place was known as 'Sheol'. This was the place where all the deceased went after death. There was no idea of heaven or hell, just a place where all the dead dwelt in the shadows.

In other periods, some tribes believed in the god in

the sky, and that the spirit of their deceased loved ones rose to live with the sky god. During these periods it became more common to build raised wooden platforms and cremate the dead – carrying the idea that as the smoke from the funeral pyre rose up to the sky, so the spirit of their loved one rose to meet the sky god.

I'm guessing that at the moment a person dies, their soul or spirit leaves the body, causing the body to become lifeless. At that point the soul enters the afterlife, whatever that is.

The rituals and practices that humans have developed around treating corpses with respect seem to have more to do with helping those left behind to process their grief than helping the departed on their journey to the afterlife.

Perhaps this morning's failure to find Brentnor Church was a symbol of this. I believe the church was there at the top of a hill. It was hidden from view by the cloud and fog. And, perhaps, what comes after this life is hidden from us by a cloud that separates the physical world and the spiritual world. Maybe we only see it when our time on Earth is done, and the time comes for us to go higher to a new place.

Yet humans from the very beginning seem to have been searching for God, for meaning, and for the afterlife. The history of spirituality is a story of cosmic hide-and-seek – a hidden God, or Truth, sought out by humankind.

oOo

As interesting as Stonehenge was, I decided not to sign up as a fully-fledged Druid.

The sun finally came out as I left Stonehenge and headed for Glastonbury.

I'd never been to Glastonbury. I've only seen bits of the Festival on the telly.

I was thinking about all this afterlife stuff when suddenly, Glastonbury Tor appeared on the horizon. It's strange how it stands so high above the rest of the landscape, which is comparatively flat.

Soon I found my B&B for the night and checked in with Tracey & Mick, the owners. Mick gave me a little map of Glastonbury, pointing out recommended eating-places for the evening.

I decided I had time to walk up to the Tor before going to find a place for dinner. I can see how people feel drawn here, as the Tor is visible for miles. And the closer you get, the more drawn you feel to climb it.

It was a pleasant evening and the sun was out. It's only a short climb up to the Tor, but it is quite steep. I'm used to hiking and walking regularly but, these days, steep climbs get me breathless very quickly.

A young couple was coming down the hill as I went up. They were having an argument – I think the young lady was annoyed she'd been dragged up a steep hill in her nice shoes for no reason.

St Michael's Tower sits at the top of the Tor, and soon I was there. The views are quite spectacular from the top. Another lone soul came up behind me and sat in the tower for a moment.

The Tor has connections with mythological stories of King Arthur, and is often mentioned in Celtic mythology.

I wandered back down the hill and into the town centre. Just as Mick's little map indicated, I found a quiet pub to get some fish and chips. Then it was time to walk back to the B&B and write up the blog for the day.

There were strange gurgling noises emanating from the plumbing. There is something unique about plumbing in Guest Houses and Bed and Breakfast establishments. No other buildings in the country have plumbing that makes noises quite like Guest House plumbing.

Another spiritual mystery to ponder...

The thing about being my age is, if you're male, two things conspire against you. First, you need to visit the loo a few times in the night, due to prostate issues. Second, your memory is sometimes impaired.

Remembering where the loo is situated when you're wandering about in the dark, in a strange room, is very important. Staying in a different B&B every night, on this trip, was going to be a challenge. Tonight, the en-suite is exactly where the wardrobe is at home. Lord help us!

6

The Lazy Gecko

'Each time you say hello to a stranger, your heart acknowledges over and over again that we are all family.'
Suzy Kassem

'I'm pickin' up good vibrations.'
The Beach Boys

Day 4 – Thursday
Glastonbury – Tenby

Deep joy. I got through the night without walking into any walls or mistaking the wardrobe for the toilet.

I got showered and dressed, and went down for breakfast.

Apart from the curious sounds from the plumbing last night, I'd assumed that there was only me and the young guy, who'd checked in at the same time, staying the night. But the breakfast room indicated otherwise.

The young guy was checking out as I got down for breakfast.

Tracey and Mick bid me good morning. Mick went off to cook my order of poached eggs on toast. I grabbed a couple of Weetabix.

A woman, who was probably about my age, came in for breakfast. Oh, other guests, I thought. I let Mick and Tracey take her order, and then we sat in awkward silence for a few minutes.

Her partner came to join her for breakfast. He looked a bit 'New-Age'. We got chatting and the lady told me that they come and stay here four times every year. They love Glastonbury. It recharges their 'batteries'.

An older American lady came in for her breakfast and seemed to have already met the new-age couple.

They asked me what I was doing and I explained the trip. I told them I was off to St Govan's Chapel in Wales, after Glastonbury, and they sounded interested though they had never been.

A young Australian lady joined us, though she hardly spoke, but mostly listened to the conversation and smiled occasionally.

Somehow we got onto family history, and the American lady told me she had been researching her family history since she was twenty years old.

Mick brought my poached eggs in and the conversation continued.

The New Age guy asked me about St Govan's chapel again and I shared a bit of the story of St Govan.

'I think that's going to be a special visit for you,' he said. 'I think it'll be very meaningful.'

Back in my room I looked at the map to see how close to St Govan's Chapel, in Pembrokeshire, I could get by the end of today. I remembered that Tenby was quite close so I booked a B&B there for tonight.

I asked Mick if I could leave my car on his drive until midday. He said I could, but he gave me directions to the local supermarket, whose car park was right near the town centre and near where I was meeting my friend.

I wasn't meeting Diana until eleven o'clock, which gave me just over an hour to have a wander around Glastonbury. I wandered along the main street and found some beautiful pavement art done with chalk. There was a shop called 'Happy Glastonbury!' which had its front window smashed in and was boarded up - perhaps not so happy then.

There were the expected crystal shops and all manner of magic on offer.

I think there are two communities at least – the older, retired, well off, Glastonbury residents, and the New Age and hippy community. I felt there wasn't much overlap with those two groups.

Like so many tourist destinations in Britain, the town centre seems a bit run down, with several vacant shops, a couple of tired looking pubs, and yet, here and there, a new shop or business just starting up.

As eleven o'clock approached I went off to find The Lazy Gecko, the café where Diana said we should meet.

I first met Diana 20 years ago when she was

exploring going into the ministry. I used to help people through that process as part of my work. She used to be a 'nightclub vicar' and for the last 7 years she's been a 'Goth vicar' in Glastonbury. She's a real vicar who lets her inner Goth come out to play. I think it's fantastic.

Almost everyone in the café seemed to know her and like her. She told me she spent the first three years here mostly listening – listening to other people's stories and narratives, rather than trying to force her narrative on others. She told me that many of the pagan or new-age stories are mirrored in some Bible stories, which enables her to have respectful and friendly conversations with everyone.

We chatted about deep theological stuff for two hours –and some ordinary stuff –but then it was time for me to hit the road. Thanks Diana, that was a great thought-provoking coffee and catch up. It's given me much to ponder. I love the Lazy Gecko café, and their coffee was great.

Inspired by my meeting with Diana, I set off for Wales with my mind doing wonderful somersaults. I had so many trains of thought but soon ran out of track.

Setting off for a long drive when your old body is expecting lunch is not good. However, I was soon on the M5 and found the services. As luck would have it, I found a KFC.

I rarely eat KFC, or any fast food for that matter. But I do like an occasional bit of deep-fried chicken.

oOo

The day was mostly dry with blue skies and sunshine. As I approached Tenby it became grey and overcast again. A few showers emptied themselves on my location.

I knew my B&B for tonight was in a backstreet, which can be a bit depressing, but the miracle of the internet means I had seen photos of my room and read reviews from people who had stayed there.

As mentioned when booking, there was no car parking at the Guest House but it was only a short walk from the station car park.

The station car park was indeed a short walk and only £1.50 to park overnight. Sadly, the ticket machine was out of order. A sticker said it was possible to pay online – so no excuse if you don't pay. There's no parking app, like the rest of Britain... so I went to the website. There was a long and torturous process – I think I even gave my inside leg measurement – but finally I had paid £1.50 by credit card.

It had started to rain during the payment process and I was getting wet again. I just wanted to get into the room and relax.

I opened the rear passenger door of the car. OK. Which box had clothes, toiletries, and snacks? Oh, those things are in several different boxes.

I'd meant to pack my rather funky hand-luggage/ overnight-case for such eventualities but I forgot to do that.

Right. Travelling tramp with a few clothes and toiletries in a Tesco bag for life it is then...

Slightly damp, I walked up to the accommodation – classy executive laptop bag in one hand, old super-market bag for life in the other hand. Yeh. I'm cool.

I was greeted at the door by Gavin.

'Hi. You must be Don. Come in.'

The welcome and the room were very good. I see why this establishment scored 9.5 out of 10 in the online reviews.

I put my 'bags' in my room and then walked into town. The sun had been shining most of the day, and despite the Welsh showers that had welcomed me, there were now blue skies. If anything, I'd felt too hot in the car today and wished I hadn't worn my jacket. Glad that the weather was turning for the better, I set off into town without one.

I've been to Tenby quite a few times, so I knew the way to the town centre. Heading towards the seafront, I left the dingy back streets behind and came upon sea views and the real Tenby charm.

Then – without permission, if you please – the heavens opened and wetness arrived. Argh! I had not even considered constant rain when planning this trip.

I walked briskly into town and came to The Buccaneer Inn. I fancied a steak and it was on their menu. Result.

What wasn't on their menu was Wi-Fi.

'Sorry we don't do that.'

In fact, not even a phone signal. I was hoping to check comments on the blog and connect with family on Facebook.

The atmosphere was nice though. Enough people to reassure me that I hadn't chosen a dive, but also few enough people to create ambience without being over-whelmingly noisy.

I was here to eat. Actually, the steak and chips was

very nice and reasonably priced.

Sadly, the walk back to the Guest House was wetter than the journey to the pub.

Back in my room, I changed into dry clothes. I checked the blog messages and wrote today's post. I messaged my friends Chris and Kate and told them I'd probably come through North Wales tomorrow, Friday, rather than Saturday, as I had previously arranged.

I continued to read the book my daughter had given me – *The Alchemist* – and got lost in the story of a shepherd boy leaving familiar surroundings and going on a quest. I felt I was on a quest, but my treasure was even less defined than that of the shepherd boy.

Tomorrow, I am visiting St Govan. He's a really cool dude. So many of my influential and 'life-guiding' friends have passed away, but maybe the spirit of one of my favourite Celtic saints would speak to me.

7

Pirates and saints

'We belong to a Mystery far grander than our little selves and our little time.'

Richard Rohr

Falling Upward: A Spirituality for the Two Halves of Life

Day 5 – Friday

Tenby – St Govan's Chapel – Shrewsbury – Talacre

As the kettle in my room quietly grumbled into life, I looked out of the window. No sea view, just the backs of the houses in the next street, divided by tiny old concrete backyards. The grey morning light struggled through dark clouds but gave a shine to the rain-soaked slate roofs. Here and there, weeds grew from leaking gutters.

I got back into bed and planned out my route while I drank my coffee. Chris messaged to say that he and Kate would be at their caravan in North Wales by 7:30 tonight, and I was welcome to stay with them.

I messaged Jackie and Howard, a couple I'd only 'met' on the internet. I'd been saying for years that if ever we were passing near to Shrewsbury, Hazel and I would pop in to see them. Well, Hazel wasn't with me, but today was as near to Shrewsbury as I was ever likely to get.

I also messaged their daughter Hannah, who I had met once before. They were available to meet a day early too, so the plan seemed to be coming together.

I went down for breakfast. There were two young guys on another table but we all ate in silence for some reason. Gavin served two perfectly poached eggs and some toast.

After breakfast, I wanted to go to an outdoor shop in Tenby and look for a new jacket. I packed my carrier bag and checked out. I remembered a little backstreet, near the shop, that had free parking, so I headed there. Unfortunately, there were no free spaces, so I circled back round and decided to head out of town. In another very narrow one-way backstreet the traffic ground to a halt. It remained stationary for some time. I got out of the car and walked down the queue of traffic. The obstacle was a large delivery lorry that blocked three quarters of the road. The driver was working as fast as he could and had almost completed his delivery. I walked back up to my car and reported my findings to the queue of waiting drivers, all anxious to know what the issue was.

Eventually the queue began to move and I was on my way. I was heading for St Govan's Chapel on the Pembrokeshire Coast. The one snag with visiting the chapel is that you have to cross a military firing range to get to it. If the army are shooting or playing war games, the road to the chapel is closed.

I passed the first warning sign about the possibility of being shot. When I got to the barrier, the gate was open and the guard post empty, so I assumed all was well. There were a couple of red flags flying along the way, which was disturbing, because that's one of the warning signs that there could be manoeuvres happening. At the chapel site there was a guard on duty in the field next to the car park, but he seemed happy with the few cars there.

The sun came out and the rain stopped. Blue skies appeared.

St Govan's chapel is reached by a very steep, and uneven, flight of steps that leads down to the bottom of the cliff.

St Govan, who died in 586AD, was a hermit who lived in a cave near the bottom of the cliff. Legend has it that he was an Irish monk, who sailed to Wales to visit the Abbot who had trained him (possibly St David). He was pursued by pirates and landed at the foot of the cliff as they chased him. The rocks opened up and he was able to hide from the pirates. Believing that God had guided him here, he decided to stay and live in a cave.

People came to visit the hermit for wisdom and guidance. There are also stories that people received healing miracles from St Govan.

In the 14th century, a small chapel was built on the site of his cave. It's said that St Govan is buried under the altar of the chapel.

I passed a retired couple at the top of the stairs. They seemed uncertain about going down the steep flight of steps. When I got down to the chapel I was the only one there. Just beyond the altar is a stone opening, leading to what is believed to be the cave where Govan lived. At the opposite end of the chapel there is an opening leading out to the rocks below and the ocean waves crashing on the shoreline.

So many Celtic saints have stories about them that include an unexpected detour on their journeys, which they then believe was God guiding them. There is something about that idea that I find attractive. Who knows which parts of the legend are true, and which bits have been embroidered? But something of spiritual significance once happened at the foot of this cliff, and the ancient chapel marks the spot.

The retired couple arrived in the chapel. The man went off right down to the ocean. His wife stood by the entrance to the chapel looking out to sea. She explained she was very unsteady on her feet and was amazed she'd got down the steps to the chapel. Her husband wanted her to go further down, across the rocks, to see the amazing sea view but she didn't think she could do it.

I went back into the chapel and looked out of the little opening that looks out to sea. The lady's husband convinced her to go further down near to the crashing waves. I heard her laugh a few times. They seemed to be having a great day.

I looked out to sea again.

St Govan, thank you that you came to this place, and

stayed a while, and imparted life, wisdom and healing.

The world so desperately needs wisdom and guidance today.

And so many souls need healing.

May your spirit give me wisdom and guidance on my journey.

May your healing spirit heal the wounds of my broken heart, as I mourn those I have lost.

Travel with me and whisper your guidance on the wind.

oOo

I climbed back up to the car park and messaged Jackie a possible time to meet up. She sent me back a postcode for a car park in Shrewsbury where we could meet. I set off across Wales heading North through the beautiful Welsh landscape.

After a while I realised it was lunchtime and I was driving in the middle of nowhere. I hadn't planned a place to stop for lunch. I decided to carry on and see if I came across somewhere to eat. I came round a bend and passed a pub that welcomed 'hikers and cyclists'. That sounded like my sort of place so I did a U-turn and drove back to it.

I ordered a bacon roll and half a Guinness. I checked the map and it looked like I was somewhere in the Brecon Beacons.

Refreshments completed, I got back on the road and headed towards Shrewsbury.

I arrived at the car park Jackie had sent the postcode for. But I couldn't see her.

I called her number and she said she was at the same car park. Just then, I saw a man walking towards me who looked suspiciously like Jackie's husband Howard.

'Are you Don?' he asked.

'You must be Howard,' I said.

We went across the car park and found Jackie.

oOo

So your mother probably told you not to arrange to meet up with strange people you only know from the internet. Well, your mother is right. Don't do it. But if you have to, always meet in a public place.

OK. This was a little bit different.

Over ten years ago, maybe even longer, my daughter convinced me to join a photography website, called Blipfoto. At the time it was fairly unique. You posted one photo a day and gave it a caption. The photo had to be taken on that day not copied from another day.

Anyway, I got to know a few of the contributors including Hannah and her Mum Jackie. We had a few private messages back and forth and began to build a friendship.

Soon we all connected on Facebook. My wife and I kept saying that, if ever we are passing Shrewsbury we should meet up with Jackie and her husband Howard.

Some years ago, I did go to Cambridge with a friend, and met up with Hannah, their daughter.

Now I was meeting her parents for the first time.

It was a shame my wife couldn't be here, but it was great to meet up with these folks at last. We walked into the town centre and found their daughter Hannah.

We went for drinks and chats in a local restaurant.

It's strange meeting someone like this face to face for the first time –yet all knowing quite a lot about each other from years of social media contact.

The sun was shining so we walked the long way back to the car through parkland. Yet again, it started to rain and none of us were really dressed for rain.

We said goodbye and went our separate ways. It was lovely to finally meet Jackie and Howard, and good to see Hannah again.

oOo

I had originally planned to come along the North Wales coast road from Anglesey towards Conway. I have so many childhood memories of holidays along this coastline. But my route had changed a lot since my original plan, and now it made sense to head straight for Talacre, to meet up with Chris and Kate.

I arrived at the site around 7:45pm, feeling immoderately peckish. I parked up by their caravan and then we decided to go out for a pub meal in Prestatyn.

The pub was packed but we did find what was possibly the last free table.

I know Chris and Kate from college days back in the 1980s. We rarely saw each other for years, as we were all busy bringing up families.

However, a few years back, one of the old gang suggested we have a reunion of the 'four amigos' along with our spouses. We've had a few meet ups with Chris and Kate since then.

Back at the caravan, Chris opened a bottle of wine and we chatted long into the night.

'A journey is best measured in friends, rather than miles.'

Tim Cahill

8

Lighten our darkness

'My soul is from elsewhere, I'm sure of that, and I intend to end up there.'

Jalaluddin Rumi

Day 6 – Saturday

Talacre – Chester – Crosby – Heysham – Torver

The gentle sound of rain on the caravan roof woke me. I got showered and dressed, and joined Chris and Kate for coffee. Soon Kate had eggs and bacon cooking as we continued our chats.

After breakfast, I got my waterproof coat from the car, and the three of us walked to the beach in the rain. I wanted to see the lighthouse on Talacre beach. I was quite excited. Why? Because this was the first lighthouse I ever saw. I was probably about six years old. We used to come to North Wales on family holidays from Manchester, where I grew up.

I have a distinct memory of just being happy and

totally absorbed with building sand castles here. I remember the sunshine, and a slight breeze. I remember looking out to sea and then over to the lighthouse. I wondered what the man who worked there was like.

Those were happy days.

I haven't been back here since I was a kid.

In my book, *The Chronicles of Godfrey*, this is where God comes on holiday. I have him staying with the lighthouse keeper, Salty Sam.

I walked over to the lighthouse with Chris and Kate and took some photos. It looks a bit derelict now but still dominates the view.

This is not a spiritual shrine for most people. It's an old shipping safety facility. And yet, there is something here that warms my soul, despite the wind and rain.

Maybe it's to do with touching the past – a past that was happy and carefree. It's like visiting my childhood – a time when my life was about things like trains and buttered toast. There is definitely food for the soul here, though in a strange unique way, perhaps personal to me.

We walked back over the sand dunes in the rain, and back to the caravan. We said goodbye and then I drove to the caravan site entrance and parked up.

I phoned a pub in Torver, near Lake Coniston, where I would head at the end of the day. They only had one room left, but it was a six-bed family room that was £110 per night. The woman told me to let her speak to the boss and she'd call me right back.

I messaged my cousin Annette and her husband Peter to say I'd be with them in Chester in an hour or so.

The lady from the pub rang back. The boss had

decided to let me have the room for £60 including breakfast, so I went ahead and booked it.

I set the satnav for Chester, and then went looking for a petrol station, as the fuel gauge was getting low again. The grey persistent rain continued for the next hour or so. I refuelled and replaced the wine gums with a fresh bag.

oOo

Soon I arrived at Peter and Annette's house and we had coffee and chats. Peter has done several road trips on his motorbike, and told me of some of the places he visited. They told me they'd been following my trip on the blog.

It was about this time, that I realised I had a bit of a following on this journey, as people were reading the daily blog posts.

I'm a member of a Facebook group about the area of Manchester I grew up in. Quite a few members were avidly reading my blog posts, and watching my progress on this journey. Family and friends were also following along. This made me feel that others were a part of my journey, cheering me on when things went wrong. It reminded me of *The Unlikely Pilgrimage of Harold Fry,* by Rachel Joyce, when a group joins him on his walk from Devon to Berwick, although that didn't go too well for him. I found it fascinating how many people said they would like to do something similar.

Soon it was time to get back behind the wheel.

I went back to the coast, this time to Crosby Beach, to see the Anthony Gormley *Another Place* statues on the beach. I was hoping to arrive here at low tide, when all the iron 'men' can be seen. Sadly, the tide was almost all the way in, and a couple of 'men' and a few heads were all that were visible.

My next stop was Heysham. This is a place I have never visited before. This stop is a bit weird ... in a lovely sort of way.

From the Lancashire coast, I'd planned to head to the Lake District. However, during the planning stage, a couple of months before I set off, I wondered if there was some sort of Celtic site between Blackpool and the Lake District. I did an internet search and came across St Patrick's Chapel – a Celtic ruin on the cliffs at Heysham. I put it on the list.

Then a friend of mine, who saw my route-plan on Facebook, contacted me to tell me her Dad's ashes were scattered there. Now that's when it got weird...

'Her Dad' was a guy called Brian, who was one of our youth leaders in Manchester in the 1970s. He became a great friend. He introduced a few of us to 'social work' – hanging out with mentally ill children at Booth Hall Children's Hospital in Manchester, as part of our community service at the youth club. Later he helped a few of us to get involved with supporting a drug and addiction rehabilitation centre in Manchester.

Spiritually, he was even more significant. He was 'the star' that led me to Christ, if I can put it that way.

Brian was a hugely influential friend and an additional father figure in my teenage years.

Sadly, we lost touch over the years. When he died, I missed his funeral – a thing I've often regretted. But this new information from his daughter meant I could at least go and say goodbye.

Or, as Sam, had said when I met her in Penzance, 'You could go and say, 'Hello.''

If I'm honest, I still didn't haven't a clue what I was doing on this trip. But things like this make me think there is something deeper going on.

I turned off the main road and found Heysham to be a small village by the coast. I found the sign for the footpath to St Patrick's chapel.

Apparently, Brian's Grandmother is buried in the churchyard that sits next to the chapel ruins. Brian loved this place and it was strange to think of his ashes being scattered here.

The view from the chapel ruins is stunning, and now the sun was shining and blue skies met the ocean at the horizon.

'Hi Brian,' I whispered, as I looked out to sea.

There was another strange thing about visiting this place I'd never previously heard of. I'm half Irish and they think it's possible that St Patrick was buried here. Patrick wasn't Irish by the way. The Irish abducted him into slavery and abused him horribly. He escaped and then ended up going back to Ireland as a missionary to those who had so cruelly enslaved him.

That's another 'weird' story.

God, 'the Universe', the 'Force', the Jedi, or whatever the heck you want to call it, seems to reach out and touch humanity in a strange way. I can't explain it but it absolutely fascinates me. These ancient places, where a footprint from the past may be discovered and touched, seem like ancient altars – a sign that God once did something here. And maybe he still is.

oOo

I left Heysham and headed for the Lake District.

Shortly after the village of Water Yeat, the A5084 meets the edge of Lake Coniston. There is a small layby and I can rarely resist stopping to take in the view that looks right down the lake, embraced by the mountains on either side.

There is an inner calm I always find in the Lake District, and I felt it the moment I stepped out of the car.

My inner calm was slightly disturbed by the middle-aged couple who were trying to load their canoe onto the roof rack of their car.

'Don't do that!' shouted the man. He was being very aggressive to his partner.

'What do you want me to do?' she asked quietly.

'No! No! No! Look what you're doing!' he yelled.

It went on like that for the next five minutes. If she has any sense, she'd leave him as soon as they get home, and find someone who treats her with more respect.

But even Angry Man could not destroy my inner peace here. I took several photos of the scene as he continued to yell at the poor woman.

It had been a long day of driving and I was looking forward to checking in and getting changed.

oOo

I first came to Torver as a teenager, on a youth club camping trip. A whole gang of us used to camp on a farm here every August. Later on, when Hazel and I got together, we came camping here together with friends and sometimes on our own.

Fond memories of those summer youth club camps are many. One very hot summer, we all camped in the upper field. The girl guides camped in the lower field by the stream. One evening it was so hot we thought we should go and cool off in the stream. The sight of a large group of long haired 'yoofs' (the boys) and short haired 'yoofs' (the girls – it was the 1970s) coming towards their camp, may have seemed intimidating to the girl guides. But our leaders soon got chatting to the guide leaders to reassure them we came in peace.

We went a little further towards the river. There was a constant stream of banter on this trip. Then someone over-stepped the mark.

'I think he needs throwing in the river!' someone shouted.

The offender was caught and duly thrown into the icy waters. Much laughter ensued.

Everyone then realised this was a great moment for revenge for various 'incidents' at the youth club over the last year. Minimal 'evidence' was shouted out and the 'jury' decided the 'defendant' needed a soaking.

Virtually, everyone was thrown in the river fully clothed. Respectfully, a few delicate people were not.

What do you do when every available victim has been duly soaked? You start again.

Soon, it was only necessary to shout a person's name

and they would run and jump in the river themselves.

The girl guides had lit a campfire and were planning songs. The leaders invited us to join them.

Wonderful. The Guides started singing:

Leader: Oh you'll never get to heaven.

Group: Oh you'll never get to heaven

Leader: in a biscuit tin

Group: in a biscuit tin

Leader: 'cos the Lord won't let

Group: 'cos the Lord won't let

Leader: No crummy ones in

Group: No crummy ones in

Chorus: Oh you'll never get to heaven in a biscuit tin, 'cos the Lord won't let no crummy ones in.

Ain't gonna leave, my Lord no more

Ain't gonna leave, my Lord no more

Ain't gonna leave I-E-I-E-V my Lord no more

Ain't gonna leave, my Lord no more

Etc...

Some of our leaders were folk singers, and soon tuned into the guide songs, developing more verses, thankfully age appropriate ones!

A lovely evening spent with fellow campers.

Another hot year, we found a path further up, through the woods, at the edge of the field, that led to a rocky waterfall with a deep pool at the bottom. We took turns daring each other to jump our hot sunburnt bodies into the icy pool at the bottom of the waterfall.

It was extremely cold – but refreshing once you were

able to breathe again.

Then there was the time Mrs E and I came here, on our own, for the first time.

It was pre-driving days, and we'd just missed the bus from Ambleside to Coniston. We could have waited two hours for the next one but we'd been travelling all day. We were carrying full-kit. All our tent, cooker, food, clothes etc, were on our backs. The rucksacks were heavy.

I suggested we walk to Coniston. Actually, in the end, it was all the way to Torver. Ten and a half miles carrying heavy rucksacks – how hard could that be?

To this day, if I ever say, 'It's just over the next hill,' to Hazel, I get the look and the reminder of this incident.

At Coniston we had just missed the bus to Torver. Trying to reassure Mrs E it wasn't very far was quite difficult. The 'just over the next hill' propaganda was wearing very thin.

Bearing in mind that Crook Farm campsite was actually just a farm, with two outside toilets and a single water tap in a field, it's impressive that we are still married.

The thing that took the edge off an otherwise brutal day was walking down to the local pub. Big log fires, great pub food, and fellow walkers and campers, and walking back to the campsite – fully fed and slightly tipsy – stopping to gaze at a clear starlit sky...

Perfick.

I could recount so many other similar stories from when life was carefree and no-one close had died.

But now it's actually now.

Some of the people I came here with, so long ago, have sadly passed away.

I've lost contact with others, and still others are suffering with severe illness.

The familiar pub even closed down.

All seemed lost.

Yet someone decided to save the pub and the memories.

And now it has rooms to stay overnight.

You may think such a venture would struggle to get customers.

You may think that but you'd be wrong. The Lake District plus bar plus good food plus log fire plus memories of middle-age people plus young people making new memories means it was standing room only. How did this place ever close?

Saturday night in Torver was pumping.

I arrived about four o'clock in the afternoon, and already the place was packed.

There's a distinct difference between checking in at a hotel and checking in at a pub with rooms. A quiet reception desk versus making yourself heard at a crowded bar.

An attractive young woman behind the bar noticed me and asked what I wanted. It took three attempts to communicate because of the noise in the bar, my Manchester/Suffolk hybrid accent, and her rather lovely East European accent.

I didn't ask her name, but wondered if she was called 'Helga'. No idea why. Except, her accent would make her a great Bond villain.

If she had shown me to my room, and been stroking a white cat, and said, 'I've been expecting you Mr Bond,' it would not have seemed out of place.

Everything seemed to become a story with her, which, as a writer, was interesting.

'Ah, you are booked into our six-bed family room,' she said consulting the booking diary.

She looked up at me.

'But you are only von person. Do you vont to book a table for dinner?'

'Is that necessary?' I asked.

'I vould recommend it,' she said.

'OK'

'Ah, Mr Egan, ve only have von table left.'

'Oh. OK, I'll have that then. About 7pm?'

'Ah, no, Mr Egan. Ve have so many customers at seven. Can you make it 7:45pm?'

'Yes, that's fine.'

She showed me to the family room.

'Ah, you have six beds! You can sleep in all of them.'

'One bed will be fine.'

'Yes. Do not sleep in other beds. It will cause us extra work.'

The pub had only recently developed the overnight room idea. The odd plastic bag with an electrical or plumbing adaptor was found around the room. There was no 'room information' folder or leaflet as in other B&Bs.

I got changed and went to the bar. It's been a really long day and a nice catch up with social media and a Guinness would be lovely.

The bar was even more packed now, but on my way in, I'd noticed a young couple sitting in the unheated garden room. I put my sweater on and took my pint in there. They were just leaving so I had the room to myself. It was a bit chilly but there were nice views and I saw everyone coming into the pub this way.

Most folks arrived in cars. However, an oldish guy arrived on a quad bike – right to the door. As he came in, I said, 'Now that's how to arrive!'

He laughed and went into the pub.

The pub Wi-Fi worked here. I was able to let family know I'd arrived in the Lakes.

The temperature was dropping rapidly. Soon, I thought I'd go in and stand at the bar. It was even more crowded now but there were a couple of empty tables. I sat down at one by the log fire. It had a little notice that said it was reserved from 7:30pm. It was only 7pm so I sat down and thawed out.

The guy who'd arrived on the quad bike was telling shepherd stories at the bar, so I assumed he was a local shepherd. I used to associate shepherding with the shepherd's crook. In recent years, walking in the Lakes and the Yorkshire Dales, I have to say that the quad bike has replaced the shepherd's crook as the sign of the shepherd.

When Mrs E and I stayed in Keld, in 2016, the local shepherd appeared several times on his quad bike, with two sheepdogs sat on the back – sign of the times I guess.

A lady came to my table and picked up the reservation card. She and her husband were standing at the bar. She came back and picked it up again.

'Is this your table?' I asked.

'No. It's alright,' she said. We're not booked in until 7:30pm.'

I stood up to stand at the bar.

'No. No. Please. I don't mean to take your table before time!' she said.

'It's OK. I've got a table booked for 7:45pm,' I said.

Helga, or whatever her real name is, noticed the incident and told me that my table was ready.

The couple smiled appreciatively and 'Helga' showed me to my table in the next room.

This room was also busy. Six twenty-something girls, who looked like they could be on a hen night or a twenty-first birthday party, were on the next table. They were loudly discussing a mutual friend who clearly had offended one of the group, although most of the group actually still liked her. Apparently.

Awkward conversations like, 'Yeh. No. I really like her, but then she said 'blah blah blah' about [insert name of important person], and I thought No. That's out of order!'

Unnecessary words and noise, in general, wind me up. So to be trapped in a noisy bar, on a table next to a group of excited, tipsy, and slightly agitated girls, is not a great place for me.

But at least they were discussing their awkward

situation. This is a healthy thing to do. I just wish that I didn't have to be on the next table to them. It was like a 'reality' TV program that I'd never want to watch. But they were generally having a good time.

I can get a bit grumpy when I'm hungry, so I had to give them the benefit of the doubt, because I'm sure that so many people gave me the benefit of the doubt when I was that age.

I recalled for a moment being in the residents' lounge in the Hilton Hotel in Nairobi, Kenya – discreet lighting, plush sofas, the international daily papers, and quiet conversation, attentive waiters. In the corner, a baby-grand piano, with a pianist tinkling out some gentle tunes. If only it could have been like that.

But it wasn't.

'Helga' arrived with a nice medium steak and chips, tomato, mushroom.

I've always found this place a quiet, log fire type of pub, but that was a long time ago. Clearly they need to make it profitable, but they seem to have been overly successful.

I like a bit of pub or restaurant ambience. I think that's what makes it. But once I feel I'm fighting for emotional survival, I want to be out of there.

Helga came and took my plate and I asked her to remind me of the breakfast arrangements, which she did.

I retired to my room and wrote the day's blog post.

I soon discovered that the bar Wi-Fi didn't reach my room. However, I could clearly see a 'Guest Wi-Fi' signal, at full strength, that did. I went back to the bar to ask for the password.

'I'll get the lady that knows it off by heart,' a young girl said.

A woman came and recited the bar Wi-Fi passcode. I told her that one didn't reach my room.

'Sorry, that's the only one we have,' she said.

I explained that there was clearly a guest Wi-Fi at full strength and asked for the password.

'Oh I don't know anything about that,' she said.

I can't begin to describe my frustration at this situation.

Full marks for installing a guest Wi-Fi that reaches all the rooms. Full marks that it's switched on. Full marks that the signal strength is one-hundred per cent.

The only thing you forgot was to put a card or note in the room – or tell your staff – what the password is. I don't know what you're paying per month for guest Wi-Fi, but you may as well flush that money down the loo.

Ninety-five per cent implemented and then the critical bit... Nah. We won't bother with that.

Here endeth the rant.

OK. Let's get back to 'analogue' living. I'll read more of *The Alchemist.* The shepherd boy was not having Wi-Fi problems. However, his money had been stolen on arrival in a foreign land, and he had to start all over again.

Yep. Wi-Fi deficiency is not really a big problem in the whole scheme of things.

9

Is that you, God?

'Before you speak, it is necessary for you to listen, for God speaks in the silence of the heart.'
Mother Teresa

Day 7 – Sunday
Torver – Coniston – Ambleside – Ulswater – Keswick

It's happened a few times in my life – that thing where you have a sudden epiphany, or it seemed God, or an internal voice, spoke. And the word or phrase seems to come from elsewhere and not from your own thinking.

The 'voice' or phrase seems to give you a new direction in life, or maybe it answers what has seemed an insurmountable problem.

Well, this morning I woke from a strange dream and, as I woke, the voice spoke inside me. It's too complicated to go into here, but it was personal to me and very affirming.

Apparently, this was the aim of the ancient Desert Fathers who went out into the desert to seek silence and solitude.

This is the aim of contemplative monks and nuns who keep long periods of silence – to hear divine guidance or a leading of the way from within.

Maybe being away, on the road, with long periods of driving in 'silence' brought this moment about. Who knows?

It felt so profound as to possibly be the culmination of my journey.

I thought about it in the shower and at breakfast. I wrote up yesterday's blog post but the Wi-Fi wasn't working at all now.

I found 'Helga' and checked out.

I gave her my credit card and she was still telling a story.

'Yes! Yes!' she was speaking to the credit card machine.

'I am giving you the card now!'

She looked at me and rolled her eyes.

'This machine is being very aggressive today. I don't know vot has upset it.'

The accent and the quirky thing of making everything a story made me warm to Helga. I know that is not her name, but I'll always remember her as that. Where was she from? What was her real name? How had she ended up in the Lake District? These were the things I wanted to ask but didn't.

I sat in the car for a moment and wondered what to do.

Should I go home? Was the purpose of the journey fulfilled?

Or maybe I should have a day off from driving and hang around in the Lakes for a day or two.

As I was thinking all these deep thoughts, it dawned on me there was a much more urgent situation I needed to deal with.

Sugar supplies were critically low. The wine gums were at a dangerous level. I'd even eaten the yellow ones, which I don't really like. All that were left were the black ones, which I can't stand. The Liquorice All Sorts were empty. The Jelly Babies had all gone days ago. If I don't rectify this situation soon, I'll be forced to open the Sports Mix, which are really for emergencies only.

I decided to drive into Coniston and find a cafe with Wi-Fi so I could upload the blog post. I found the cafe I remembered from a previous visit, with a sign in the window saying 'Free Wi-Fi'.

I got a coffee and opened my laptop. Sadly, like so much 'Free Wi-Fi' in cafe's and bars, it didn't work.

I finished my coffee and went back to the car. I was still feeling really undecided as to whether I should carry on, go home, or hang a round for a few days. I got in the car and then realised I needed to top up snacks and drinks. I tried to find another parking space but Coniston was already packed with visitors.

I turned down a narrow lane that heads up to The Old Man – the hill of that name, not an actual elderly male. But all the parking spaces were taken. The lane gets narrower the further you go. Soon it was too narrow to turn round so I had to continue upwards.

The road then runs out of tarmac and turns into gravel, as it gets much steeper. I had to engage four-wheel-drive to stop the wheels from spinning, but I felt rather smug that I had that option. Eventually the road levels out and widens just before the old slate mines.

I stopped and got out to take in the view. I could sit in the hills of the Lake District all day just taking in the view. It's such an inspiring place.

I guess this is what happens when you are very unde-cided about where you're going. You find new places and revisit places you forgot about.

Sometimes you find yourself in the middle of nowhere, and sometimes in the middle of nowhere you find yourself.

I turned the car round and drove back down to Coniston. As I couldn't find a parking space I drove on to Ambleside.

I parked up and walked past the little house on the bridge, into the centre of town. I found a pub and ordered some lunch.

I was still feeling restless and uncertain about whether to continue, when a friend called me to let me know that someone we had been praying for had lost her battle with cancer and had passed away – another dear friend gone far too soon and too young.

I forgot about buying snacks and walked back to the car. It began to rain quite heavily and I hadn't come in a coat. As it rained, it somehow symbolised the many tears that would be shed for the loss of my dear friend.

I thought of her husband and daughters facing such a tragic loss. My heart broke for them.

oOo

Clearly, at my age, I will encounter friends, loved ones and even relatives passing away, more frequently than when I was in my twenties. However, that only makes me think more about the issues around death and bereavement.

Someone asked me recently, 'Are you alright?'

I haven't been anywhere near alright since my Mum died in 1984, aged fifty-six.

Dad died the same year aged fifty-seven.

When our son died a couple of years later, just before his third birthday, I was pretty much trashed mentally and emotionally.

I don't think I've ever recovered from those three rapid losses, despite many conversations and, more recently, professional counselling.

I don't make close friends easily. I'm more towards the introvert end of the scale. We prefer depth and trust with a few friends, rather than sheer numbers of friends.

Sadly, several of my closest man-friends have died in their early fifties.

Emotionally, I am one of the walking wounded. I think too deeply about loss, bereavement and funerals. I wonder if funerals are more for those left behind than the person in the coffin.

It seems to me, if we do have a soul – and I believe we do – it leaves the body and goes on to the next life at the moment of death.

So having a ceremony, a week or more after the person died, seems to be more about helping those left behind cope with the loss, or showing respect for departed.

And that is good.

Sometimes we carry coffins or ashes to special places, connected with the deceased. Again, I think that is more about our resolution rather than the comfort of the person we lost.

This is all rather dark, and I really hope I have not stirred up uncomfortable feelings for anyone reading this. It's just been a very unwelcome, recurring theme of my life.

It was a struggle back when my Mum died in 1984.

It was another struggle today to hear of one more friend – such a lovely young soul – who was taken far too soon, and without whose light the world will be much poorer and darker.

oOo

Ironically, I left Ambleside via *The Struggle* – also known as the Kirkstone Pass. It's a steep and bendy climb through breathtaking scenery. As soon as I began the climb up the pass, the rain stopped and blue skies and sunshine appeared.

Part way along *The Struggle* I was flagged down by two young ladies. They told me they'd been on a big family walk but one of the kids couldn't manage it. The dads had turned back with the little ones, and the two mums had carried on alone. However, the route was far longer than expected so they were asking for a lift to the top of *The Struggle.*

I laughed and said I'd love to help, but I've got so much of my own junk in the car that there wasn't any room.

'Perhaps you could just take one of us and then we can collect the one left behind in our car shortly,' they said.

I told them the passenger seat was pushed all the way forward and I couldn't move it back because of the 'bed'. 'But, if you think one of you can squeeze in, I'll happily take you to the top of the hill.'

So one young lady did a contortionist act and squeezed in and off we went.

Soon we reached the top of *The Struggle* and she extracted herself from the car and joined the rest of her family. I assume they went back for the other lady.

I continued on towards Ullswater, stopping occasionally to take in the views.

The traffic came to a standstill about a mile from town. There was a long wait with no traffic moving in either direction. Eventually, the traffic started moving again but very slowly. Soon I saw the reason why. A car and a motorcycle had collided. The motorcyclist was sitting in the road looking very dazed, surrounded by passers by trying to help. Some were attending to the injured man. Others were directing traffic.

It's horrible how you can set off on a nice day out and end up involved in an accident by the afternoon. I hoped everyone was OK.

I arrived at Ullswater and paused by the side of the

Lake for a moment, still unsure where I was heading.

The loss of my friend, and then seeing the road accident, gave me a heavy heart and added to my indecision.

It is in these moments that having a plan, however far I had deviated from it, meant there was still a route sketched out. Perhaps the right thing to do is to just continue on my journey and see what happens. And maybe that's what we have to do in life sometimes.

I thought of the little shepherd boy in the book I was reading, who listened to the wind, and twists of fate, hoping to hear the voice of the Earth leading him on.

My next proposed stop was Friar's Crag, at Derwent Water. They say it's the best view in the Lake District, so I went and checked it out.

oOo

The view is rather wonderful. A little boy and his sister were having a whale of a time at the edge of the lake. Their young parents stayed on the grass and watched them, occasionally shouting instructions to them.

I had imagined coming here alone and taking the view in with only birdsong for company. But after the sadness of today, there was something wonderfully refreshing about hearing children laughing and running about excitedly. The 'newness' of small children and their simple view of life often makes me smile. And perhaps I was longing for the carefree days of my own childhood.

Looking across Derwent Water from Friar's Crag, the ancient landscape stands reflected in the still waters of the lake – the majestic mountains surrounding it, and the canopy of blue sky that reaches down to the hilltops.

We humans come and go, but the place where we once lived and walked remains forever, and gives life to the next generation, even after we, ourselves, are gone.

oOo

Walking back to the car, I decided it was time to go and find my accommodation for tonight. Soon I was in a narrow back lane in Keswick and found the address. I drove up the steep drive and parked the car. Eight very colourful VW Classic Campervans were parked up at the property. Apparently part of the business here is campervan hire.

I rang the doorbell and Diane, a lovey friendly soul, answered the door and welcomed me. She showed me to my room and then asked if I'd like a coffee. I said yes and she served a cafetière of rather lovely decaf, along with a few almond thins.

She recommended the pub just round the corner for an evening meal.

After enjoying the coffee, and letting Mrs E know I'd arrived at the next stop, I got changed and went to look for the pub. I was ready to eat.

Unfortunately, Diane was right – it is a lovely pub serving great food. So great, in fact, that there was standing room only, and not much at that. Absolutely crowded.

I decided to walk into Keswick and find something there. I walked right along one side of town and down the other side. All I found were pubs and restaurants with over-priced pompous menus. You know the type of thing – 'Organic free-range avocado, marinated in unicorn tears, on a bed of wholegrain chickpeas, served on a chopping board – £45.99'.

Plates! I want a plate! What is wrong with the world?

Finally, I found a pub that had plenty of space. It was fairly quiet. The staff were friendly, and the food was good, and reasonably priced. In addition, they served their food on plates. Ten out of ten!

I had gammon, egg and chips with peas, or, as the other places in Keswick would have described it, 'A generous char-grilled slice of hand-reared pork, accompanied by free range corn fed poultry ovum, with triple cooked potato batons, and the fruit of the Pisum-sativum climbing plant, all served on preheated ceramic circular crockery, with genuine Sheffield steel cutlery, and ethically sourced paper gob wipe'.

OK. Maybe not the last bit.

The banter between the two barmen and the young waitress was epic – an entertainment in its own right. The Guinness wasn't bad either.

And... good Lord! Their Wi-Fi worked and was quite fast. Why isn't everyone in this pub?

More customers came in and, the problem with being a lone traveller is that, if you pop to the loo, your table will have been taken over by the time you return.

Anyway. Probably time to walk back to my accommodation.

When I'd walked into town it was still daylight. Now, on my return, it had got dark.

No problem. Walk by the river out of town, turn right when the river does, and just before a roundabout with streetlights, turn left up a narrow unlit lane.

What could be simpler?

I followed the river. I turned right with it. I passed the really nice pub – that now had free tables – and then saw the streetlights on the big roundabout. I kept looking left, for the little lane up to my B&B. Ah! Here it is.

Wow! This unlit lane was darker than I had imagined. No worries. Just keep on walking on the road. I came to the first house. It was bigger than I remembered and on the opposite side of the road to the houses I'd seen on the way down.

The house was really big... There's the double garage security light coming on.

Ahead... only darkness.

Oopsie. This isn't the lane. This is a rich person's drive. They could let the dogs out at any moment! (I'm a bit scared of dogs.)

I turned and walked very fast down the drive. I pulled out my phone and tried to locate myself on the map app.

Oh. Hang on... No. I really am on the right track. Now I can see where I am despite the darkness.

I turned again and walked back up the lane. The temperature had dropped and I was starting to feel the cold.

No problem. Soon I'd be in my nice warm room.

I looked down at my phone to follow my progress on the map app. The blue dot assured me I was on the right course...

Then... it suddenly jumped to the left of the lane I thought I was on.

Arrrgh! I am in someone's front garden!

Another U-turn and walking back down the drive as fast as possible without actually running.

I came out of their garden and aimed between where I had just been and the well-illuminated roundabout.

Groping my way through the darkness, I gradually found the actual lane I was looking for. I used the light from my phone to see the way.

Soon, back in my room, calm was restored.

Most of my online messages were from a Facebook group I'm a member of, about Newton Heath, the area of Manchester I grew up in. There were calls to 'support me' as I was one of their own. But I wasn't fundraising, or walking, or cycling, or anything demanding. But they seemed very engaged in the story of my journey.

The Chairman of the Cricket Club said that if I got to the club, on my journey, the drinks were on him. I had no idea where the cricket club was, but, if he was offering to pay for a round, I thought it worthy of an internet search.

A few other members were saying that if I came through Newton Heath – as I planned to – they'd love to meet me.

I'd love to meet them, as some were old primary school friends, and others just grew up at the same time, in the same area.

oOo

I was planning to head to Gretna Green tomorrow, and then over to the East coast, to Lindisfarne. Much too late to think about that, but I was starting to think that several friends, who'd advised me to go up the West coast and come down the East coast, may have been wiser than my planned route. Maybe, like the little shepherd boy I was reading about in my book, I needed to listen to the wind, the omens, and my heart.

It had been a joyous, wonderful, disturbing, profound, sad, and, almost, bewildering day.

Sleep beckoned.

I complied.

10

Alone

'The best part about being alone is that you really don't have to answer to anybody. You do what you want.'

Justin Timberlake

'Being alone and actually sitting with our own thoughts can lead to such growth and realizations that are rare in our everyday busy lives.'

Kourtney Kardashian

Day 8 – Monday
Keswick – Gretna Green – Oban

At breakfast there was only one couple in the dining room, apart from me. I thought back to the lovely conversation I'd had at the B&B in Glastonbury. I wondered about striking up a conversation.

Unfortunately, the couple argued for over half an hour about telegraph poles and the UK broadband network.

No.

Really.

I couldn't help but hear.

Yes.

You are in the Lake District, sunny day, view of hills out of the window, someone else made you breakfast... and you want to argue about telegraph poles and broadband coverage?

It didn't seem to matter what he said, she held the opposite view. It became so irritating, after a while, I finished my breakfast and went back to my room to plan my day.

I'm realising I put far too many stops on my route plan. It could take a couple of months to do them all.

It was partly the fault of being unclear about what the purpose of the trip was. Was it a photography holiday? Was it about visiting distant friends? Was it an actual pilgrimage? Was it really about the inner journey into the soul?

Unsure of the answer to any of those questions, I decided to head North of the border.

I put the coordinates for Gretna Green in the satnav and set off. Soon I was on a rare stretch of motorway I had never driven on before. I've travelled a lot, around the world but also to most places in the UK. But now I was in uncharted territory. The motorway was fairly quiet. This was rather good news for the two cars I came across. One was smashed into the central reservation, the other, a wreck on the hard shoulder. Mercifully, all occupants seemed uninjured and one guy was on his phone, presumably phoning the police or a recovery vehicle.

I'm driving thousands of miles on this trip. I passed my test in 1980. I've driven all kinds of vehicles from small hatchbacks to the largest removal lorry you can drive on a car license. I have been an angry impatient driver in the past, and still have the odd moment. However, in my fifties, I became the oldie driver. The guy that often drives around town at twenty-five mph, sometimes to the annoyance of other road users.

But I am well aware that, however good a driver you are, it can be other people, or unexpected emergencies, that cause accidents. A tyre blowout at speed, a driver having a heart attack, drunk drivers, drivers falling asleep at the wheel – any of these things can, and do, happen on our roads.

Thankfully, the three collisions in my driving history all happened at under fifteen mph.

Nevertheless, having bought a brand new car that was now only a year old, I'd rather not have any accidents, even the ones at low speed.

The satnav told me to take the next exit, and soon I was back on local roads and then arrived in Scotland. The moment was marked by arriving at The Old Toll Bar – The First House in Scotland.

I assume this was an old toll house, from the days when deeply rutted, unmade roads were maintained by charging a toll at certain points to any who wanted to travel along that route. Turnpikes and toll houses were ended in the late 1880s, when responsibility for road maintenance passed to local councils.

These days, the idea has returned for things like the Dartford Crossing, the M6 Toll road, and toll roads in France and other parts of Europe.

As interested as I was to go in and have a look at the bar menu, I was heading further. However, the loos were discreetly accessible from the rear of the building, and needs must, when you are fifty-nine-and-three-quarters and have a dodgy prostate.

As I returned to my car, there was a guy in full formal Scots clothing – kilt and all – getting into his car. I wondered what function he had been to that a kilt was the appropriate dress.

oOo

A little while down the road I came upon The Old Blacksmith's shop at Gretna Green – a place of legend.

Runaway marriages, where underage couples ran away to Gretna Green to get married, started around 1754, when an English law was passed that meant you had to be twenty-one years old to marry, or have the permission of your parents.

The law applied to England and Wales, but not Scotland.

In Scotland, boys of fourteen and girls of twelve could marry without parental consent.

Scottish law meant that, if a declaration was made before two witnesses, almost anybody had the authority to conduct a marriage ceremony. The blacksmiths in Gretna became known as 'anvil priests' – the most famous such blacksmith was Richard Rennison, who performed 5,147 ceremonies.

I followed the signs to the car park, though I just wanted a quick photo here. I parked up and, although it was not high season, the place was bustling with tourists. There were souvenir shops, coffee shops, and places to eat but it was far too busy and crowded for me. I went and took some photos of The Old Blacksmith's Shop and was ready to get back on the road and escape the crowds.

But then... I heard bagpipes.

I've just arrived in Scotland.

Yesterday was an emotional rollercoaster.

But someone is playing bagpipes.

I walked towards the source of the sound.

There, in the grounds at Gretna Green Blacksmith's Shop, was a guy in full formal Scottish regalia, including the kilt and a bearskin on his head, playing the bagpipes.

As I got closer, I saw it was the guy I had just seen in the car park at the The Old Toll Bar.

So that's why he was dressed up.

Nearby, there was an old milk churn with a wee Saltire fluttering in the wind.

'For the piper', the notice read.

He was good.

I got quite emotional. I know that's the plan – to make an emotional connection with the tourists, and extract the maximum amount of money, especially from the wee Sassenachs.

And yet, he played as well as he dressed.

I'm trying to listen to the wind, the omens, the Spirit, and my heart on this journey. And my heart was telling me that Scotland welcomed me on my journey. The pipes were calling from glen to glen to say they had been expecting me.

I put a couple of my Sassenach pounds in the donation box.

When the piper paused to get his breath back, I had a wee conversation with him. I said that his bagpipe performance was quite a grand welcome to Scotland. He asked me if I was on holiday. I told him a bit about my journey and that I'd come up from Land's End.

He nodded his head sideways and said, 'Aye, that's quite a long drive.'

Slight understatement.

oOo

Soon I was back on the motorway and pondering what I was doing. I still felt that life, the Universe, God, or whatever, was pulling me and leading me on this journey.

I am used to seeing motorway signs with familiar place names like London, Manchester, and Newport Pagnell.

However, the next turn off was signposted for Lockerbie. A place forever etched in my mind in connection with the 1988 bomb that bought down a jumbo jet here. It was such a sad event in our nation's history. Horrible.

oOo

It was way past lunchtime and I needed something to eat. I pulled into the next services. It was absolutely crowded. Yet again, I'd romantically imagined I'd find a quiet place to have a coffee and a nice meal.

No.

It was pretty much low quality fast food all round.

Except I saw a Harry Ramsden's fish and chip shop outlet.

Now the word 'outlet' in that last sentence should tell you all you need to know. But I do like fish and chips.

In Manchester, where I grew up, Harry Ramsden's had a great reputation. It may still have. But old Harry sold his Yorkshire chip shop business in 1954 – three years before I was born – for £37,500. It was sold on again in 1965 to Essex-based Associated Fisheries.

Essex.

No offence, but that's not Yorkshire.

Or Manchester.

The experience was far less than pleasant – almost fighting to get a table, pressure to 'go large' at the point of sale, and the meal bore no resemblance to the marketing photographs – true of too many places today.

Over-promised and under-delivered.

In the early years of the motorways of Britain, motorway services were the sort of places where people went out for a meal. People drove to motorway services specifically for a high quality night out – hard to imagine today. I find today's motorway services to be very stressful places, clearly designed to be 'get them in, extract the maximum amount of money, and then get them out again' sort of places. I loathe them for valuing profits so far above good customer experience.

I'd like to turn up to find a quiet jazz bar with table service – someone playing jazz piano on a grand piano in the corner. Sofas and discreet lighting should be involved. Newspapers on a large coffee table would be provided. Thick carpets and no piped music would be the order of the day. The dream of going to the loo and finding quiet, soft lighting, and proper towels, rather than loud tinny music and advertising, with noisy, alleged, hand-driers that make a lot of noise but never dry your hands.

It's highly unlikely that I'll ever be appointed as the 'Minister for Motorway Services Development', but if I ever was, within a year, every traveller in Britain would adore me.

Maybe not that last bit, but all your long journeys would far less stressful.

Eventually, I was off the motorway and up into the highlands of Scotland. I passed by the 'bonnie, bonnie banks of Loch Lomond', which brought back memories of that song on the radio when I was little.

It may have looked 'bonnie' if it were not for the grey sky, persistent drizzle, and general atmospheric gloom.

I've seen the Lake District at its very best on a few holidays, when glorious summer sunshine lights it perfectly. Once you've seen a place at its best, it's easy to forgive its worst days.

But I'd never passed this way before. I was seeing the highlands on a poor day. Not at their worst – that would be under six-feet of snow with impassable roads – but a poor day nevertheless.

But were the rain and the gloom speaking?

What were they saying?

What was my heart saying?

My head was saying, 'Just get on with it and reach

the next B&B!'

I fought against that and stopped many times and got my proper camera out to take photos. But the damp conditions drove me back to the car every time.

I was feeling quite flat. Maybe it was the sad news of yesterday. Maybe it was the atmospherics. Maybe it was just that I was a long way from home and missed my family.

And yet, this is a thing. This is quite an awesome thing. Who else does a trip like this? Who overcomes all the obstacles and follows their dreams and convictions and does this?

'This' being driving from your home... to your home, via the longest and most inconvenient route.

After what seemed an age, I arrived in Oban. The old Victorian Terrace B&B was right on the quayside. There was a council car park at the end of the building. I'm sure I'd seen something about free parking when booking.

I gathered some belongings into my carrier bag, whilst dreaming of the expensive hand-luggage/overnight bag I had intended to bring.

Unpleasantly moist, I climbed the steep steps to my accommodation. I rang the reception bell. Eventually, a tall unshaven man appeared. At first he seemed unhelpful. I told him I had booked a room this morning.

'Are you trying to tell me something, Pal?' he said, like some drunk looking for a fight in a Glasgow pub.

'No. I booked a room. On Booking.com...'

He looked me in the eye.

'Aye, alright then.'

He looked in the booking diary.

'Right, Pal. You're in room five. Top of the stairs and turn left. How you payin'?'

He'd extracted funds from my credit card before you could say 'Nicola Sturgeon'.

The room had been renovated to a high standard, and there was a nice view over the bay. I went back down to ask him what time breakfast was and any recommendations for tonight's meal.

'Breakfast? That's not a thing we do. There's lots of places for breakfast though. There's a Wetherspoon's.'

OK.

So not a B&B then... Just a B.

Journey of a lifetime – breakfast in Wetherspoon's?

Not really feeling that.

He recommended a bar a couple of doors down for the evening meal.

Was it the rain?

Was it this guy's unwillingness to provide anything resembling 'service'?

Was it tiredness?

Was it being nearly sixty?

Who knows? But I was feeling pretty low.

I got my waterproof coat out of the car and went for a walk around the town. I'd only come here because I saw the town featured in a program on the telly. It made it look very picturesque.

The reality is more of a run down seaside town with boarded up shops and grim streets. It has an amazing backdrop of Scottish hills and a view out over the bay, but it felt just like a hundred other struggling towns in

Britain.

Having not found anywhere tempting to eat, I settled on exploring the cellar bar two doors down from the B&B, or rather the B.

There was only one other customer, and the place looked like it had seen thousands of packed nights heaving with drunken clientele.

The young couple running the bar were really friendly and there were cosy booths around the main bar. In moments like these, a pint of Guinness and a good steak often lift the spirits.

They did.

A few more people came in and the free Wi-Fi did actually work – ten-out-of-ten for this place.

More than could be said for my accommodation.

Tomorrow I will wake up and be sixty years old. I never thought I'd last this long or be this old.

I remembered what my 83-year-old friend, Keith, said when I told him I'd be sixty – 'Enjoy your youth!'

Thanks, Keith. I suspect that is good advice.

Yes. Let's enjoy the journey.

Once again, I sensed my dear departed friend, Martin, laughing and saying, 'It's all about the journey, Don.'

I was feeling a bit homesick now and wished I could fast-forward the trip, but I know that's not the point of it. So I'm trying to learn something from each day and each experience.

On my last day of being fifty-nine, I am going to sleep.

Night all.

'There are two mistakes one can make along the road to truth – not going all the way, and not starting.'
Buddha

11

The Long Dark Lunchtime of the Soul

'I may not have gone where I intended to go, but I think I have ended up where I needed to be.'

Douglas Adams – *The Long Dark Tea-Time of the Soul*

Day 9 – Tuesday

Oban – Loch Ness – John O'Groats

Well, there may be no breakfast in this establishment but at least there are coffee making facilities in the room. I popped the kettle on and opened the curtains.

A blue sky stood as the backdrop to the bay, with its deep blue waters and the majestic hills. Blue skies always lift the mood.

Some people expressed sadness that I was spending my sixtieth birthday alone. But they needn't have worried. I don't like parties much. I value silence, personal space, and time to think. So perhaps this was a birthday gift to myself. We can do the family tea party another day. But today is a day I want to think and reflect.

I sat in bed with my coffee and looked at the map. Where should I head for today? There were lots of possible stops, mostly to see breath-taking landscapes. The weather was still very changeable though.

I could possibly make it to John O'Groats if I pushed it.

The thought made me smile. Although this is a circular drive, I did want to tick off both Land's End and John O'Groats along the way. Land's End had been done earlier in the trip. John O'Groats was within reach.

I got the app up, on my phone, and found a little B&B that seemed to be located quite near to John O'Groats and booked it. Now I was committed.

Time to think about breakfast. I could just go and find a café. I could go to Wetherspoon's. But I was getting tired of cafés and bars. I have food in the car. I could go and get some milk and just have some coffee and cereal.

I found the local Tesco and bought a pint of milk. I set up my little camping table that attaches to the back of my car. I made coffee with a flask of hot water from the 'hotel' and had a bowl of cereal.

Yes, I did get a few strange looks from passers-by. One lady smiled and said, 'That's really neat!'

'So, Don, how did you spend your sixtieth birthday?'

Well, it started with having breakfast in a Tesco car park in the Scottish Highlands...

I washed up the breakfast things and packed them in

the storage boxes.

I checked the map again. I could probably make it to Loch Ness by lunchtime.

This high up in the Highlands it gets fairly wild and, here and there, new vistas of beautiful scenery surprised me round every corner.

The rain held off for most of the journey with the odd shower breaking through.

The roads are narrow but fine, as long as you don't get stuck behind a slow lorry.

I got stuck behind a slow lorry.

Eventually I passed and continued on my way.

On the approach to Loch Ness I came to some temporary traffic lights on red. One of the workmen came over to my car.

'Sorry, Mate. We've got four-way control and we've had to put them all on red because we're right next to a swing bridge, and it's being opened to let a boat into Loch Ness. Last time that took 15 minutes. So you're in for a bit of a wait, I'm afraid.'

Deep joy. I switched off the engine and waited as the queue behind me stretched back to England.

Eventually I was on my way again. I was getting a bit hungry so I headed for Urquhart Castle, on the shores of Loch Ness, as I knew they had a café from when I last visited. I got stuck behind another slow lorry for several miles but I wasn't far from the Castle and lunch.

The satnav was showing I was close, and announced that I was half a mile away.

And then...

STOP.

Everything stopped.

A police bike came by with blue lights flashing.

I could see reflections of blue lights beyond the lorry but couldn't see what was happening.

Then another police bike went by...

Twenty very hungry minutes went by...

And then... I saw the monster! Two of them in fact. I saw them with my own eyes.

No. Not Nessy. But the two longest loads I have ever seen on British roads. I don't know what they were carrying but they were really long. Wind turbines possibly. How the heck had they got these things down these small roads?

I got to Urquhart Castle and had a very nice tuna mayo and cucumber butty.

I've been fascinated with Loch Ness since I read about the monster legend as a little kid. I suspect what really keeps the legend alive is the discovery that the story brings tourists who, in turn, bring money into the local economy.

Loch Ness contains more fresh water than all the lakes in England and Wales combined – a mind-boggling fact.

oOo

Back on the road, I got stuck behind another wide load travelling North at about 29mph. After twenty minutes of this torture, I managed to overtake and get on with my journey.

With a few miles to go, I came over a hill and was greeted by a rainbow. I know it's just caused by atmospherics but I want to 'listen' to nature on this trip. Somehow it felt like nature was smiling and happy about my journey. Call me sentimental or stupid. Whatever. I thought it was a lovely welcome to the middle of nowhere.

The road seemingly goes on forever, and I had moments of self-reproach today:

'This is the most pointless thing you've ever done.'

'Why am I going to John O'Groats? There's nothing and no one there!'

'This is a really pointless part of the trip!'

'You are wasting a ton of fuel and money and polluting the environment just because you're mad!'

The Dark Night of the Soul, I think they call it.

I had almost been expecting it.

There always comes a moment on the journey where doubts creep in and try and take control. Self-doubt rears its ugly head. The critical inner-voice starts nagging.

There is little you can do about this, except be determined to press on through the negativity, hoping it will pass.

The howling gale and frequent downpours were not helping.

The nearer you get to John O'Groats, the more 'end-to-enders' you spot. A lone and soggy hiker with a huge backpack, a cyclist with overloaded panniers – these are the brave, or foolish, souls really going from one end of the country to the other. What stories will they be able to tell when their journey is completed? And, more interestingly, what inspired them to do the journey in the first place?

The road up here is long, lonely and mostly straight. Now and again, you reach a few buildings at a road junction that form a small community in this unforgiving landscape.

The constant gale-force winds blow salty spray off the sea, so nothing but heather grows here. It makes the landscape look desolate and forgotten.

'Take the next right,' said the satnav. I followed orders but was still in deep thought.

'Take the next left.'

I was now on a narrow single-track road in the middle of nowhere.

'You have arrived at your destination.'

Erm. No. I don't think I have.

Where I'd arrived was a little farm track in the middle of nowhere with two sheep chewing grass, and looking at me as if to say, 'Another stupid Sassenach lost in the Highlands...'

I drove on for a bit, but the precious few buildings I found were either derelict, or clearly private homes.

I'll have to phone the owner of the B&B, except there is no phone signal here. Why would there be? Hardly anyone lives here!

I drove back to the main road and found a signal.

I explained to the owner that I'd turned right at Keiss. This was difficult, as I didn't know how to pronounce 'Keiss' without sounding like I was saying 'kiss', and also because English was not the owner's first language.

Finally, he understood and directed me back to the main road. He told me there was a sign at the end of the lane.

Sure enough, I saw the sign and turned down the right lane this time.

Marco greeted me and checked me in. A biker had arrived just before me, and it was normally Marco's wife who showed people to their rooms. But she was out. He seemed a lovely, gentle guy who paid attention to detail. He explained how everything worked, and about places nearby to get an evening meal.

The room was spotless and had a hint of Greece about the decor – a good find.

Apart from the hurricane blowing outside, all was quiet. This was good news and what really I wanted after five hours on the road.

I got changed and then back out into the gale. There was enough daylight left to drive five minutes down the road to John O'Groats to take the obligatory selfie, with the famous sign. Trying to get out of the car at John O'Groats, I almost lost the car door to the elements. The wind was even stronger here. I found the sign and took some photos. Apart from a couple, and their teenage daughter, the place was deserted. Perhaps everyone else had just been blown off the cliff.

For many people John O'Groats marks the end of their journey. For me it means I'm about two thirds of the way. There is still a long way to go.

I drove out of the car park to the pub Marco had recommended. As he said, it looked shabby on the outside but inside it was fine. There was a double-glazed storm porch at the entrance that felt like the airlock on a space ship. You had to fight your way in and get the external door closed, before you opened the inner door at the other end. Opening both doors may have resulted in everyone in the bar being sucked out of the door into the gale.

My hairstyle now resembled that of Ken Dodd. The bar was silent. Four men, who appeared to be locals, sat at the bar each with a pint. No one made eye contact with anyone else. No one spoke. No one even looked in my direction. I wasn't sure if one of these guys was the barman or not. Somehow I felt the need to break the silence.

'A bit breezy out there!' I said.

Three of the men didn't move a muscle or respond in anyway.

The old boy at the end of the bar slowly looked in my direction.

'Aye' he said gently, and then went back into his own world.

How the heck do you order food here?

Mercifully, a young barmaid, with the ability to speak a whole sentence, appeared and took my order. I found a table and waited for my steak and chips to arrive.

Steak and chips, with a pint of Guinness, two nights running – this may have been comfort eating.

A group of six people came in and broke the silence

with normal pub chatter. For me, it was time to get back to Marco's place and write up the blog.

I got an early night and was just going off to sleep when I heard a loud strident voice downstairs. Either another guest had just arrived from Glasgow, or Marco was married to a loud-talker.

Eventually silence was restored.

12

Far from Dull

'It is better to travel well than to arrive.'
Buddha

Day 10 – Wednesday
John O'Groats – Dull – Aberfeldy

I woke to the sound of the loud-talker with a Glaswegian accent. The whole house had no carpets – everywhere was either tiled or had wooden flooring – so the sound did travel a bit.

I got showered and dressed and went to find the source of the noise, and breakfast.

Gina is lovely. But she is a loud-talker and borderline long-talker. I kept expecting her to say, 'See you, Jimmy!' But she didn't because she's a person, not a stereotype.

The biker guy was checking out early. The only

other person at breakfast was a young woman who mentioned her fiancé and her ex-boyfriend in equal measure. She was up here on business and asked me what I was doing. She told me of some of her journeys to different parts of the world.

Extracting myself from the dining room was not straightforward, as Gina and Marco went into their double act, with Gina doing most of the talking. I got the story of why everything is more expensive in the Highlands, why her free-range hens produced much bigger eggs than you can get at the supermarket, and stories of young end-to-enders she'd let camp in the garden.

I got away in the end. I packed my carrier bag and tried to check out but, unfortunately, I got involved in another conversation. Another guest was a lorry driver on his way to deliver a prefabricated garden office. He was extolling the virtues of his company's garden buildings, when Gina made the mistake of saying it would just blow away if it was in their garden.

The guy put his bag down – always a bad sign – and went into the full technical reasons why it would not blow away. Marco finally processed my card and I was eager to get on the road. The four of us stood in the small hallway and unfortunately I was positioned furthest from the front door. At a rare moment when Gina paused to breathe, I tried to manoeuvre myself towards the door.

The lorry driver had paid, and he was now the only thing standing between the door and me. They went round repeating the same 'Thanks for everything,' and the corresponding, 'Do come again'.

The lorry driver opened the front door, I was almost free, but Gina mentioned his garden buildings again. The guy was blocking my exit and went over his sales pitch again. Every phrase had already been said twenty times!

Just open the blinkin' door! I thought.

Finally, I was outside.

I wanted to check the map and set up the satnav before I got on the road, but now Marco and Gina were outside the house, and I couldn't risk getting drawn back into another conversation. I drove down the lane and onto the main road. I found a small layby and pulled in. As I looked at my route the wind was shaking the car quite violently.

Tomorrow morning, I hoped to meet up with my friend Kerry in Dundee, so I was aiming to get most of the way there today. I'd booked a hotel in Aberfeldy and hoped to arrive in good time. However, I noticed that a place called Dull was a short distance from Aberfeldy, and I've wanted to go there for some time. I first heard about Dull when I came across a book called *Far from Dull: and other places*, by Dominic Greyer.

The book is a collection of black and white photographs of strange, amusing, or rude place names. If you want to smile and laugh for ten minutes, and make your friends do the same, I highly recommend it. There is a photo of the welcome sign at Dull on the front cover. I thought it would be amusing to take a selfie at the sign.

I needed to replace the wine gums and snacks, so I headed for the nearest supermarket. I came to ESCO. I found that ESCO is very similar to TESCO, except the letter 'T' had blown away in the constant gale-force winds.

oOo

I've struggled with this Scottish part of my journey. At first I couldn't work out what the problem was. Then it struck me that I don't have any memories or connections here. Even though my friend Kerry lives in Dundee, my connection with him is from college days in London and when he lived down the road near Cambridge, a few years later.

It was interesting to go right to the top of this island we live on, but I just don't feel any connection here. And, now I have another day without meeting up with anyone. Maybe these few days are more about the inner journey rather than the geographical one.

Monks and nuns are well-practised in silence and contemplation – the tools of the inner journey.

What is the inner journey?

I guess it's about knowing yourself and also trying to connect with the source of life, which some people call God.

It's about reflecting on our life-journey, our strengths, our weakness, perhaps where we made mistakes and how to possibly rectify them.

It's about working on ourselves, to bring about self-improvement and fulfilment.

It's about finding wisdom that we can apply to our own situation.

The recent surge of interest in 'mindfulness' is also connected with the inner journey. The practice of becoming still and silent, of listening to our own breath as we breath more deeply – all these things can help us know ourselves and possibly draw closer to God.

Religions use the word 'prayer' for the idea of becoming still and turning our inner gaze upon the divine light.

Sometimes the inner journey becomes uncomfortable as we uncover aspects of our 'shadow' or dark side. This is why many avoid looking inward – they don't want to see the unpleasant parts of themselves.

We may disturb old emotional wounds or upset our inner child.

So the inner journey can be just as joyful or difficult as a geographical journey.

Each person's inner journey will be unique and deeply personal. But most of us are looking for a deeper peace or some sort of healing for our soul.

oOo

A few miles down the road, I came to Badbea, a former Clearance Village. I had always thought the Highland Clearances were about the English throwing peasant farmers off their land. But here at Badbea, I discovered the wealthy tyrant, who caused so much suffering and pain, was a Scot. It was the old story of the rich abusing the poor. The rich man wanted to start intensive sheep farming, so he drove all his tenants off the fertile land. They ended up on a clifftop, open to the elements, on land where only heather would grow.

As I walked around the ruins, I noticed rectangular strips of land that were green, in contrast to the purple heather. Apparently, these green strips of land are where the poor had hand-ploughed the hard ground to try and grow a few potatoes and other crops.

There is a constant gale-force wind here and a sheer hundred-foot drop down to the sea. The people who lived here had to tie their livestock, chickens, and sometimes even their children, to the house to stop them falling, or being blown off the cliff.

The people have all gone and the ruins, a monument, and patches of green ground are all that physically remain of this sorry chapter in history. No doubt a lot of bitterness remains in some of their descendants.

oOo

Next it was on through the Cairngorms mountain range where there were still areas of snow up on the tops. I stopped now and again to take in the view and to reflect on my journey.

Hours later, my meditations were interrupted by the satnav – 'Take the next right.'

What?

I was fairly sure I was on a motorway, so there couldn't be a right turn. It turned out it was an A-road and not a motorway, and there was, indeed, a right turn. Suddenly I was on a single-track road winding across heather-covered moorland, without another human soul in sight. The road snaked on for mile after mile, with some ridiculously steep and sharp hairpin bends.

After another hour or so, I came across the 'Welcome to Dull' road sign. And, to be honest, that's all I had come to see. There isn't much at Dull, though St Adomnán is buried here. He was the cousin of

St Columba who was an Irish abbot and missionary credited with spreading Christianity in what is today Scotland. St Adomnán succeeded him as Abbott of Iona.

The place-name 'Dull' may mean 'meadow' in Gaelic.

Dull is twinned with Boring, in Oregon USA.

No, really it is!

oOo

A short drive later, and I arrived in Aberfeldy for the night. It was the best accommodation of the trip – five stars.

The last couple of days had been very long drives. After checking in, I went back down to the car and sorted out some fresh clothes. It became apparent that the dirty laundry was building up and I found a bin liner and started putting all the used clothes in it.

I'm now running low on quite a few items. I think before tomorrow's meeting with Kerry, I need to find some T-shirts, undies, and a new pair of jeans.

The hotel had a rather nice residents' lounge on the first floor and I settled in there, with the laptop, and wrote up the blog post for the day.

A small beer made the moment even better.

An hour later, I took my place in the restaurant and had what was possibly the best meal of the trip. It was only another steak really, but so obviously cooked by a proper chef. Everything was cooked to perfection, the steak was juicy and the pepper sauce was to die for.

I had an early night and continued to read *The*

Alchemist and follow the fortunes of the young shepherd boy on a very different journey.

13

Desperate Dan

'To travel is to take a journey into yourself.'

Danny Kaye

Day 11 – Thursday
Aberfeldy – Dundee – Norham

I woke to blue skies and had a rather wonderful breakfast in the restaurant.

I did a web-search and found that there was an ASDA in Perth that had a clothing section. I reckoned I could get there and make my purchase and still be on time for my meeting with Kerry.

I found the clothes I needed but, although it was still early morning the checkouts were all busy. Then I noticed a lady at a counter. Three-foot letters announced this was Customer Service. A sign nearby with six-foot lettering read 'Happy to help!'

The lady was wearing a bright yellow jacket with the

words 'Happy to help!' emblazoned on it. As she was unoccupied and had no customers, I thought she could checkout my five items of clothing.

'Just these,' I said.

She stared at me.

'You'll have to use the checkouts. This is Customer Service,' she said.

Hmmm.

Well, actually I am a customer. I was also asking for service. And the signage implied you'd be happy to help.

That's what I wanted to say.

But obviously I just sheepishly took my things and joined one of the long queues.

So, not really 'Happy to help,' at all.

Able but unwilling to help, may have been a more accurate slogan. And the desk should be renamed 'Customer disservice'.

I do dislike the commercial over-promise and under-deliver experience. Why raise our expectations only for us to have them dashed in reality?

I chucked my new things in the back of the car and headed for Dundee.

oOo

'Call me when you are outside the house and I'll come out and help you find a free parking spot,' Kerry had messaged me. He lives in downtown Dundee, quite near the town centre.

I called him and he came out and suggested I drive round the block and he would walk and help me find a space. I could see what he was thinking – there's a narrow lane that runs behind his house that has free parking. However, on this day, his neighbours and those in the know had taken all available spaces.

I stopped the car and adjusted the sectional bed platform, so that I could push the passenger seat back to allow him to get in.

'OK,' he said, 'We can drive to the beach and have coffee there.'

We parked up near the River Tay, Scotland's longest river, and had a walk on the beach.

It's strange, isn't it – I rarely see this guy these days, and yet we picked up the conversation like we were back in the coffee bar near the college at Blackheath, in London, where we first met thirty years ago.

Kerry has been a significant influence in my life.

I have to say, when our son died in 1987, during heart surgery, just before his third birthday, I don't know what I would have done without this guy. He came to the Coroner's office with me to get the 'cause of death' papers, after the autopsy, and then on to the Registrar's Office to get the Death Certificate. It was one of the hardest times in my life, but this guy stuck with me and helped us through that dark time.

He was also the guy who made me believe in myself.

We walked along the beach for a while in deep conversation.

Kerry took me to a glass fronted modern structure overlooking the beach. We sat in the front window and ordered coffee. We continued to chat at a fairly deep level, gradually realising that this was a beautiful, hot, sunny day in Scotland, and we were effectively sat in a greenhouse with our aptly named sweaters on.

Kerry suggested we go to the museum in the centre of Dundee for lunch and I was happy to escape the heat of the beach café.

We parked my car near his home and then walked into the town centre.

We walked past a large old building and he told me it was the D C Thomson building, where the Beano and Dandy comics were designed and produced. This was amazing news. Not only did I deliver the comics on my paper round when I was a teenager, I subscribed to both publications back in the 1960s.

Kerry pointed out that Dundee School stood immediately opposite the building where the Beano was produced. The artists and writers looked out onto the school playground everyday. This is believed to be the inspiration for the Bash Street Kids. It was an amazing moment in my life.

As the infomercials always say, 'But wait! There's more!'

It turns out William Wallace – aka 'Braveheart' – also went to Dundee School, not the current building, obviously, but on this site. So that technically makes William Wallace one of the Bash Street Kids.

That thought alone, made this trip worthwhile.

We walked further into town and said hello to Rabbie Burns, or, to be precise, his statue.

When we got to the museum, Kerry was keen to show me the skeleton of a Celtic Christian woman. We chatted about how different her journey of faith was in comparison to a present day person.

A more simple faith, of a person without access to books, the Bible, tapes, CDs, podcasts and the massive stream of information we have today. Possibly even very little access to a priest or teacher. It would have been her and her God, whom she heard from through nature, circumstances, and life events.

We had a lovely lunch in the museum and put the world to rights. I had possibly the best tuna mayo and cucumber butty... in the world.

Kerry shared some stories of his recent visit to the Holy Land and what a huge impact it had on him – to walk the streets that Jesus walked, and wander along the shores of the Sea of Galilee, and several other amazing experiences. I was a little jealous. I'm unlikely to make that trip myself but it was a privilege to hear of the encounters from a friend.

I felt I should get back on the road, but Kerry suggested a little detour on the way back to the car.

We turned a corner and met a couple of very old friends. There before me stood a life-size statue of Desperate Dan from the Beano comic. Just behind him was Minnie the Minx. This was fantastic.

Dundee has some very sad areas. But it also has some great areas. The beach along the riverbank of the Tay is amazing on a sunny day like today. The whole idea of statues of Beano characters and those from other publications like *Oor Wullie* just made me smile.

It was wonderful to see my friend Kerry, who was once an angry orange-haired punk-rocker, but is now a pioneering vicar and a Canon of Dundee Cathedral. Above all, like me, he's just a guy trying to make sense of life.

It was time for me to head South. This involved sitting in rush hour traffic infested with road works.

Deep joy.

There's a line in the 1960s Goon Show where Neddie Seagoon explains the reason for the road works.

'This is part of the government's dig-up-the-road-to-confuse-the-traffic plan,' he says. Over fifty years later, old Neddie Seagoon still sounds plausible. Can it really be true that, in our day, every road improvement scheme vastly underestimates future traffic flow?

It is in these moments that the wine gums come into play. Other 'drugs of choice' were unavailable, but a sugar overdose seems perfectly acceptable to society. I may have eaten a whole bag of wine gums, except for the yellow and black ones – I just don't like them.

Eventually, I was on a long quiet road and eager to get to my destination.

I could hear Martin saying, 'It's all about the journey, Don,' but road works and drives that are too long are not where I usually find my inspiration, except back in the day, when Martin was in the car with me.

I came to a really long road with lots of straight sections and very little traffic. The temptation to overtake slow vehicles and just go for it was huge. But I noticed old speed cameras positioned in all the places you could safely pass. I kept to the speed limit as I passed each of them. And then, when they seemed to have all gone, I overtook a slow lorry on a long straight stretch or road, and then noticed an old grey speed camera as I flew by.

You may think I was exceeding the speed limit. I couldn't possibly comment.

To date, I have received no penalty notices in the

post. Thus 'proving' that I remained under the legal limit.

I rest my case.

A few hours later, I finally crossed the River Tweed, and the border, back into England. It seems that no passport is required at the moment. There's just a small discreet sign with a little St George's flag emblem, and the word 'England'.

I was glad the pub I was staying at, in Norham, did bar meals. It had been a long drive, and the last thing I wanted was to have to search for a place to eat.

When I got to the pub where I was staying, the lady behind the bar told me they didn't do food on Thursday nights.

My heart sank.

She explained this was because the Fish and Chip van came on Thursdays, so they gave the chef the night off and allowed customers to bring their chip suppers into the pub and even provided cutlery.

I took my bag to my room and then ordered a Guinness in the bar. As she poured the Guinness, she explained that the when the Fish and Chip van arrives, a lengthy queue builds rapidly.

A few locals came in and chatted about things.

I wrote up my blog post, and my notes for the day, The barmaid told me the van had arrived. I took my laptop up to my room and left my Guinness on the table by the coal fire.

I went to investigate tonight's food-source.

There was already a queue forming but I got in at a reasonable position.

There was 'Haggis & Chips' on the menu, which tells you how close to Scotland I still was. I'd probably not go for that even North of the border. South of the border, I still think that's a 'No'.

I ordered fish and chips and soon I was served. I retrieved one of my sporks from the car – a spork is a bit of travel cutlery that is the shape of a spoon but with a fork end and a serrated edge down one side, thus serving all cutlery needs.

Back in the pub, one of the locals had taken my table, even though I'd left my Guinness and my sweater as an indicator that the table was taken.

Too tired to cause a scene, I retreated to the next table which was a bit of an afterthought of a table and made me feel a bit second-class.

More customers came in and it soon became apparent that there was a ladies' bingo event in the other room. I am a bit sensitive to noise and my room overlooked the main entrance. I wasn't sure how late the bingo would go on.

After I'd finished my meal, I moved to the window seat at the front of the pub, and finished writing my notes and blog post. There was a great atmosphere and, clearly, many of the customers were locals who knew each other.

One of the old boys in the bar was a lorry driver. He soon became a bit sweary, as he recounted tales of lesser mortals than him using the road. Don't get him started on people who call the Jeremy Vine Show on Radio Two.

The barmaid clocked off for the night and the evening girl clocked in. As she left, she said, 'Hey, Don, what's your Facebook or blog address for your trip?'

I wished the blog address was simpler. I told her what it was, but who knows if she ever remembered or had a look?

(It's donsdriveblog.wordpress.com if you're interested in the 'live feed' I put out at the time of the trip – you can see pictures from the trip too).

Soon, the bingo started next door and I decided to retire to my room, which unfortunately was right above the bingo room.

I checked messages and Facebook. There were now a handful of people saying that, if I came through Newton Heath – the area of Manchester where I grew up – they'd love to meet up with me.

It did seem a good idea, on this trip, to visit the street where I grew up, although our house has long gone. To meet up with old school friends and strangers who'd become fans of the journey seemed like a lovely thing to do.

The bingo ended at nine-thirty and by ten o'clock the place was fairly quiet.

Tomorrow I wanted to get onto Lindisfarne Island, and off again, before the tide cut me off. I re-checked the tide times and planned an early start.

Time and tide wait for no man.

Soon I was in bed reading more of *The Alchemist* and the story of the shepherd boy on his epic journey to the pyramids.

14

Grasping his ghost

'Ever has it been that love knows not its own depth until the hour of separation.'

Khalil Gibran

Day 12 – Friday

Norham – Lindisfarne – Newcastle – Flamborough Head

The sunlight peeping round the edge of the curtains, the sound of doors being opened, footsteps, and occasional plumbing noises – these are things that stirred me from my sleep, as morning came to Norham.

I made a coffee and thought about the day ahead.

Was I rushing my journey with today's plan? I was heading to Lindisfarne first. It's a place I have visited a couple of times. The first time, Mrs E and I parked on the mainland and walked across just as the tide had gone out. We didn't realise that, following the road, it's a three-mile walk. By the time we got there we only had a couple of hours before we had to set off back across the causeway before the tide came in.

On the second visit, we drove across and let the tide trap us on the island. We visited the castle, and then found that everything, except the little gift shop, closes around half-past-two in the afternoon, so we couldn't find anywhere to eat.

What I keep meaning to do is to visit here for a day or two, perhaps on a retreat. To soak in the story of St Cuthbert and visit the place where he prayed.

I thought I may do that on this trip but I'd arranged to meet my friend, Ian, in Newcastle later today, so it was going to be a short visit of maybe an hour or so, on Lindisfarne.

oOo

I got chatting to another couple at breakfast who told me they like travelling around Britain and using B&Bs. They asked a few questions about the trip, and also told me of some of their journeys.

Once I'd packed up and checked out, I typed 'Lindisfarne' into the satnav. But it wasn't listed. I tried to find a postcode for Lindisfarne on my phone but to no avail. The panic began to set in because the tide times dictated when I could and could not cross to the island.

I remembered visiting the village of Seahouses when I last went to Holy Island, and was fairly sure that was very close. I typed that in and found it. When I get near Seahouses, I'll see the signs for Holy Island and turn off.

I was aware that time was ticking away as I drove. Then I suddenly came upon Bamburgh Castle. Oops!

I'm very sure this is quite a bit South of Holy Island.

I pulled into a layby and got the map app on my phone to connect. Yikes! I was way off course. I managed to get the phone app to set a course. Now my inner Basil Fawlty was coming out. Driving faster than I normally would, I retraced my route back up the coast.

I found the causeway and raced across to the island car park.

Walking as fast as I could, I headed to the church and the ruins of the priory.

This really is not the way to experience Holy Island. This was the first moment when I began to think that my original idea of doing this trip is small sections, at different times throughout the year, may have been better. However, there is definitely something to be said for doing it all in one trip. I just didn't want it to be this rushed.

What I was trying to tune in to was the thing of just letting events and situations lead the way. If my plan wasn't working out, it may just be bad planning on my part, or maybe it was the universe guiding me.

Having told Ian that I'd see him in Newcastle at lunchtime, I didn't want to mess up his day.

In the short time I had, I tried to tune in to the peace of this place, and the story of St Cuthbert.

St Cuthbert was a slightly eccentric hermit who lived on Holy Island, who later reluctantly became a bishop after being urged by the King, before retiring back to his hermitage. But his version of faith was far more artistic, creative, and free-thinking than the prevailing trend. Soon it was over-ruled by dogma and conformity from Rome. That was the day we lost a huge resource of goodness. Bring back Cuthbert, I say, or, at least, his more creative version of the faith, at any rate.

The Vikings invaded here after Cuthbert passed away, and they caused a lot of damage. The monks, who had followed Cuthbert, had to flee with his corpse, to protect it from desecration. The incident is remembered in the church with a life size woodcarving.

oOo

The clock was still ticking. After an inappropriately high-speed tour, it was a race to get off the island before the tide came in. There are countless tales of motorists having to be rescued because they underestimated the challenge of four feet of rapidly rising seawater. I don't want to be one of them.

I reached the mainland safely, before the tide was fully in. I pulled over and gave Ian a call to let him know my arrival time. It was good to hear his Geordie accent again after so many years. He told me to call him when I reached his block of flats, and he'd come down.

An hour or so later, I arrived at Ian's tower-block and gave him a call. He emerged from the entrance.

Twenty years has passed since I last saw Ian in person. I could see that he now walked with a stick, and he struggled, a little bit, to get in the car as my 4x4 is a bit higher off the ground than smaller cars.

'Well, I'm in but I don't know if I'll be able to get out again!' he laughed.

He gave me directions to a local café and a car park nearby. We ordered a couple of egg and bacon butties and some drinks. 'Wey aye man, like!'

We remembered old times and Ian introduced me to the owner of the café, who was clearly a good friend of his.

I knew Ian had been ill a while ago but only now did I discover the seriousness of his illness. He'd gone to bed on a Saturday night. When he didn't show up at church the next day a friend went and called on him. But there was no answer. By Monday people were getting worried and they went to see someone who had a spare key to Ian's flat.

They found him still unconscious in bed. He had been suffering from a nasty virus, which had now infected his brain.

With the ambulance crew thinking he'd had a stroke, he was taken to hospital. He remained mostly unconscious for sometime. The virus had been so invasive, he had to learn to walk and talk again from scratch. This had obviously taken several months.

But now he was back, living independently, and only needing a walking stick to aid his walking. That's quite a recovery.

I met Ian over forty years ago when he was one of the chaplains of Strangeways Prison in Manchester. I did some work with the chaplaincy at Strangeways and later spent six weeks working as a trainee chaplain in Wandsworth Prison, in London, during my training.

Ian was a stepping-stone for me going into ministry.

He was also leading the service in the chapel, at Strangeways jail, when all hell let loose, and the infamous riot started – an event that was extremely traumatising for everyone involved, including Ian.

Ian has translated his skills of helping young offenders find their way in life into setting up an asylum-seeker project in Newcastle.

Movingly, he told me of a young boy, whose dad had been killed in one of the recent wars that refugees are fleeing from. The boy was seventeen years old and said, 'It's not right that a seventeen-year-old boy doesn't have a dad. Will you be my Dad?'

'Yes. Yes I will,' said Ian.

He was used to standing up in court for young offenders. Now he stands up in court for asylum seekers. He has spent his life standing up in court for young people suffering injustice.

Most people would be intimidated by Home Office lawyers. Ian is not.

One of the barristers he goes to court with says her day is always improved by having Ian as a witness.

There's a national shortage in our day of positive father figures. I think it specially affects young boys. With few role models, they can grow up angry and unruly – the wounded child within cries out for love. Sometimes they find affirmation in gangs, or in radical religious groups. If group affirmation is all they can find as a second-rate substitute for a father's love, they will often make do with it for a season.

The importance of people like Ian, quietly living out his ministry, and being a father to the fatherless can hardly be overstated.

I left Ian in town as he was going to get some shopping. I set off towards Flamborough.

Twelve days of long drives and strange beds were

starting to take their toll. What also troubled me was the route plan had now become so vague I couldn't identify anything that could be described as the end.

The written plan had been abandoned near the start of the trip. Now I was trying to listen to my heart, or the universe, or whatever.

I was thinking of going to Manchester tomorrow, to the street where I grew up. I could meet up with some of the locals from the Facebook group who'd been following my journey on the blog.

Then I was going to go back to the Fylde Coast to see friends.

This trip began with an inner voice, or feeing the 'pull'.

Well, today, I felt the pull, or heard the voice again.

I think I'm done.

Whatever this trip was about, I think it is almost completed.

Almost.

oOo

I arrived at Flamborough Head, and thought about how it was here that I had first talked about the idea for this trip with Martin. This had been his place.

I drove right down to the lighthouse that stands on the clifftop, and parked the car.

I walked out to the headland, where Martin's ashes have been scattered. You come to a fence that's there to stop you walking past it, to the unstable cliffs beyond. Martin always stepped over the fence as if it were a stile, beckoning him further. I always pointed out that the fence was there for a reason.

I was going to stand at the fence because that's the 'safe' and 'sensible' thing to do. But I felt drawn on by the memory of the wry smile of my lost friend. He would often sit right out on a little mound at the top of the cliff and watch nature, often early in the morning. I think it was his happy place.

I careful climbed over the fence and slowly walked along the very narrow footpath round to the far side of the cliff.

I found the little mound where Martin used to sit. Four of us sat here about two years ago, like a scene from *Last of the Summer Wine*, and chatted about life.

Back then, my friend Adrian had shared something profound a monk had said to him – 'God is not else-where.'

I remembered those words as I sat down.

My emotions were all over the place.

I laughed.

Then I cried.

Then I smiled.

I've lost too many close friends and family.

These days, I try to be thankful that, for a while, they were part of my life, and I was better for having walked with them part of the way. I think that's better than dwelling on the bitterness of loss.

In a way, I'd come to say 'Goodbye' – to get closure – but I've got into the habit, on this trip, of saying, 'Hello'.

Yes.

I could go on further on this trip and meet more

people and have more adventures, but no.

I think I'm done.

Well, almost.

This is where this mad idea was first talked about.

Maybe this is a proper and appropriate place for it to end.

Sort of.

There is just one more very special person I want to meet on this journey.

Tomorrow, though.

We're all tired now.

Tomorrow, I'll head home.

But by then, home and I may have changed.

'We shall not cease from exploration. And the end of all our exploring will be to arrive where we started and know the place for the first time.'
T.S. Eliot

15

Going home

'I was born a long way from where I belong and I am on my way home.'

Bob Dylan

Day 13 – Saturday
Flamborough Head – Spurn Point – Stowmarket

Today felt awkward. I wrestled inside between wanting to go home and continuing the journey.

I was the only guest at the B&B, so breakfast was eaten in silence. Well, apart from the country and western music coming from a little CD player in the dining room.

I packed my aged shopping bag for the last time and checked out.

I set the coordinates for Spurn Point to meet up with one more person, before heading off home to Suffolk.

Although I said yesterday that the trip appropriately

ended where the idea started – at Flamborough Head – nevertheless it obviously ends at home, because it was always a circular trip. But I needed this little detour.

It took a couple of hours to get down the coast to what seemed another lovely 'middle of nowhere' place. The satnav said I'd arrived but I couldn't see the motorhome that my fellow 'gypsy traveller', Sharon, lives in.

I messaged her and she gave me directions, and I soon found her standing on the road. Her motorhome was hidden on a farm.

In this book, I mention losing my dear friend, Martin, to cancer just over a year ago. Martin was Sharon's husband. She bought a motorhome last year and has been on a far more epic journey across Europe, all the way to Portugal and back.

It was great to see her again and catch up about our respective journeys – both the geographical ones and the journey through life.

We had a coffee while Ebony, Sharon's dog, wagged her tail for a while then settled down for a nap, as Sharon and I continued to talk.

It's strange that in all the years I knew Martin I only met Sharon a few times. It's really been in more recent years that I got to know her a little bit better. Sadly, what unites us more now is the loss of Martin.

I have nothing but admiration for Sharon, in the way she journeyed through the dark times of Martin's cancer, often carrying the family, and deeply loving her husband to the very end, and beyond.

She is a star. She'd probably deny that, but she is. I

see a gentle soul and a fellow soldier of life, who shares a similar wound of grief and loss.

As I got up to leave, Ebony sprang back to life and wagged her tail.

We said goodbye and I got in the car once more. There were lots of little lanes and villages to pass through before I reached a fast road.

Eventually, I came to the Humber Bridge, and memories of crossing here when visiting Martin, during hospital visits and home visits, before he died, flooded back.

God, I miss him so much.

I hadn't thought about lunch really as I was absorbed in my thoughts. Then I realised I was approaching Doncaster Services, which has a Gregg's. I got a craving for a corned beef pasty.

I'd stopped here almost every time I'd visited Martin in his last days, and knew the rest of the journey would be done almost on autopilot.

oOo

So what was this journey about?

It was possibly an attempt to break my routine and do something very different – an attempt to find the route to the next season of my life.

Maybe part of it was to follow Martin's advice and see what happened on this trip.

There has been an element of soul-searching as I've travelled.

It has also been about processing grief and loss.

It has been experimental, and meeting people along the way without an agenda has been refreshing.

It has been a pilgrimage. In one sense, it was touching places from the past that were significant, and visiting others for the first time to see what happened.

But maybe the real pilgrimage was the journey inwards. Perhaps it was about visiting my inner child to reassure him all would be well. Yet, the tables were turned. In the end, it felt more like the inner child, who was whole, was the one reassuring the present day me, with all my emotional baggage.

The idea of a whole, or holy, child, bringing peace in darkness, sounds a lot like the Christmas story.

Both in the inner journey and the geographical journey brings me back to the idea of Namasté – 'I bow to the divine in you.'

The people I met along the way, who showed me kindness and friendship – not only the friends I met, but people I met in B&Bs, shops and on the streets – I see something of the divine spark in them. Though they themselves seemed unaware of it.

In the end, I visited my own soul and reassured it of the available goodness towards it from others.

oOo

Several hours later, as I turned into the street where I live, Spring seemed to have sprung. The cherry-blossom tree on the corner was in full flower.

I backed the car onto the drive and switched off the engine. Journey's end.

Since I left home two weeks ago, I have driven 2,742

miles. It's been quite a journey and given me lots of memories of the adventures, places, and people I met along the way.

I see something in myself and in others now that I didn't see before. There is, indeed, a divine spark in the human soul.

So, to your soul, and to my own soul, I say, 'Namasté.'

'It's all about the journey.'
Martin Garner

Can you help?

If you liked this book, will you do me favour? Please leave a review on Amazon. It will take you less than five minutes. This really helps me and will help others find this book. Many thanks.

Connect

Twitter: @Don_Egan
About Me: http://about.me/donegan

Made in the USA
Lexington, KY
06 May 2018